Peter's poetry speaks to who we all know we're capable of being, but we just aren't quite there yet. His words are uplifting and give us that extra nudge of support that makes a big difference when we need it the most. This book is a true gift!

Melissa Curling, District Dance Studio Director

This book clearly reflects Peter's unique and masterful gift of inspiring and motivating others. The positive tone and empowering concepts are conveyed in a creative, relatable, and well-organized fashion. A great read!

Diane Kern, Ph.D., Creator of Happy and Healthy U, LLC: "Learn to Love Life and Live Well" Series

Peter Colwell is a master of the written and spoken word. He inspires the reader to think of attitude as the fuel that drives the engine of life, moving from negative self-talk to personal and professional success. He offers numerous examples through the Emotional Scrooge (boundary management), the Snark Shark (beware of toxins), and the Chronically Cantankerous (itching for a good fight) to make his point. Peter, as poet, embeds his own sage advice throughout each section, convincing his reader that attitude is everything. What a pleasure it was to read this exceptional book and to refill my own tank!

Sharon M. Weinstein, MS, RN, CRNI-R, FACW, FAAN, CVP, DAIS, CSP
Chair, National Speakers Association Certification Committee
Chair, the Healthcare Businesswomens' Association
Coaching/Training Program
Past President, NSA-DC

Life can be difficult to navigate, especially when negative thoughts distract us from fulfilling our purpose. In this thoughtfully crafted guide to creating upswings in our lives, Peter shows us how to positively confront challenging people and situations, be selective with our words (which carry weight and influence—for better or worse!), and grow from every experience life puts on our path.

Bill Cates, Author,
Beyond Referrals and *Radical Relevance*

East Boston native Peter Colwell shares encouraging poems, thoughtful quotes, and various personal vignettes filled with hope, perseverance, and the ability to always see the positive resolutions in difficult challenges. Something we can all do by finding gems within this book! Bravo! I am sure his mom—to whom he dedicates this masterful craft—and his dad are very proud!

Sherri Raftery, M.Ed., Professor, Toastmaster,
doctoral candidate, doctoral dissertation author:
"Foster Youth Mentorship Programs in Higher Education"

Peter Colwell is a poet with a purpose to lift attitudes, inspire hope, and affirm the spirit of God within us. Adversities, setbacks, and disappointments are opportunities for us to choose hope over despair. Peter has beautifully blended poetry with prose woven with possibilities of what can happen when we invest in shifting our attitude.

Helen Holton, CPCC, PCC, D.Min.
President, National Speakers Association—DC Chapter

INVEST IN YOUR ATTITUDE

Creating Upswings During Downturns

PETER COLWELL

Germantown, Maryland

Disclaimer:
This book is intended to provide practical ways to live a better life. It in no way serves as a substitute for professional counseling or therapy. Every effort has been made by the author, editor, and publisher to produce a complete and accurate book. The purpose of this book is to motivate and inspire. The author and Dreams Unlimited Press shall have neither liability nor responsibility to any person or entity with respect to any loss or damage caused, or alleged to have been caused, directly or indirectly, by the information contained in this book.

If you do not wish to be bound by the above, you may return this book to the publisher for a full refund.

Invest in Your Attitude
Creating Upswings During Downturns
by Peter G. Colwell

Published by:
Dreams Unlimited Press
13034 Mill House Court
Germantown, MD 20874 U.S.A.
peter@petercolwell.com
www.PeterColwell.com

Design by: TLC Book Design, *TLCBookDesign.com*
Cover design: Monica Thomas; Interior design: Erin Stark

ISBN 978-0-9717268-1-9
ISBN 978-0-9717268-2-6 (e-book)

Printed in the United States of America.

In Memory of
Marjorie Virginia Colwell

My wonderful mom

(1938 - 2020)

It is a rare and beautiful blessing to have two extraordinary parents whose love, commitment, and dedication to each other are equaled by their care and concern for their children and grandchildren.

I was fortunate to have my mom in this world with me for forty-five years—to be nurtured by her and to be loved by her as a child, adolescent, and young adult. And then, to develop a real friendship with her as a grown adult—going on vacations every summer and confiding in her on important life decisions, health scares, and general "what should I do now?" advice. My mom shared in the joys of her family, and she prayed fervently for us when times were tough. She never stopped believing in us and held us in the highest esteem.

It was the honor of my life to be able to spend time caring for her in her final weeks of life in the summer and fall of 2020, before she succumbed to pancreatic cancer. The final song I sang to her on her last day on Earth was "It Is Well with My Soul":

> "When peace like a river attendeth my way, when sorrows like
> sea billows roll, whatever my lot Thou hast taught me to say …
> It is well, it is well with my soul."

When I finished the song, she said: "That was beautiful. OK, you can let me go now."

As I declared during my words of remembrance at her funeral: "Mom, we are letting you go, but we are holding you very tight in our hearts."

In Honor of
Peter Gillen Colwell

My wonderful dad

An apple doesn't fall far from the tree. I am proud to have a father who has nourished me with faith, hope, and perseverance—and a love of the written and spoken word. From my earliest memories, we have gathered together as a family—singing songs at the table, telling jokes, making up tongue twisters, and having a jolly good time celebrating life! Enthusiasm is my dad's middle name!

My dad is a prolific writer, has an exuberant voice, and has a passion for entertaining and uplifting others. His passions have certainly rubbed off on me—and hopefully some of his talent has as well! I wouldn't be where I am today without his solid advice, his loving-kindness, and his belief in me. No matter how steep the climb or how daunting the path, he always *knows* I will find my way. My dad is always ready to share a story of how he overcame a similar challenge, and to encourage me to stay the course.

Thank you, Dad! I love you!

Special Thanks to ...

Bob Erdmann, my foreign rights literary agent, whose communication with me spurred me to action to finally complete this book.

Michelle James, my Creative Emergence Coach, for bringing light and awareness to my emerging talents and creative abilities—a process that has led, in no small part, to the creation of this book.

Brian Kelly and **Prashant Koirala,** long-time friends and mastermind partners, who encouraged me year in and year out to "remember the dream" and pursue it.

Mike Matthai, my "brother from another mother," who reminded me that I was already living my dream when I thought I was still merely pursuing it. The pieces were coming together, and you helped me realize that.

Carol Stauffer, my cheerleader and co-developer of corporate leadership programs to make a difference in people's lives. What a joy it has been to create and deliver workshops with you! And to gain national recognition together for our leadership development and new-hire onboarding programs! Wow!

Peter Merrett: Who knew that one hour on Skype with you would bear such wonderful fruit for my speaking and writing career? And result in your ongoing coaching and encouragement through the ups and downs of life? A hearty "thank you!"

Sheila Thibodeau, **Andrea Glasco**, and **Synina Pugh**—for your steadfast friendship through the years! What we experienced as coworkers was so special and unmatchable! We are fortunate to be able to celebrate each other and reminisce "the good old days!"

Sue Kravitz, a long-time friend who has always encouraged me in my creative pursuits! You've known about this "book in the works" practically since its inception, and you have been nothing but a positive influence on me and my career!

Marc Kravitz: Thank you for helping me build my "word power" as my constant "Words with Friends" companion!

Dr. Diane Kern—a kindred soul. So glad our paths crossed one December afternoon at a workshop on wellness during the holidays. Our similar styles and approaches have overlapped so well over the years. Your support and feedback have been spot on!

Yahya Asfoor—a rare gem of a human being. Our friendship began on a basketball court at the Real Estate Games, a charitable event to fund the effort to find a cure for Type I diabetes. It continued on through a series of meaningful conversations that have enhanced our friendship over the years. We keep pushing each other past adversity, knowing the sweetness of patience and endurance to help us reach our most treasured goals!

My fellow Speaker Academy graduates: Michael K. Jackson, Cathy Richards, Paige Trevor, Ginger Moran, and Frank DiBartolomeo—your insights and feedback have contributed to my growth and development as a speaker and writer!

Peter Vogt, my editor and friend, who patiently waited until the manuscript was ripe—allowing events in my life to unfold at their own pace, adding richness to the content of this book. You helped me position this book to align with my core message!

SPECIAL THANKS TO ...

Tami Dever, **Erin Stark**, and **Monica Thomas** of TLC Book Design—what a joy to work with you all again, after nearly twenty years! Boy, has the publishing world changed over the last two decades, but your kindness and compassion haven't missed a beat!

Kathie Carrigan, my mom-in-law, who encouraged me to take my speaking show "on the road." Thanks for your belief in me and your support of our family!

Susan Boriso, my sister and loving supporter through life's ups and downs. Thank you for rooting for me ... every step of the way!

Petey and **Vanessa**, my beautiful children, for believing in me and having no doubt that this book would be brought into the world! You are—and always will be—my pride and joy!

Trevia-Lynne (Mango Mama, Tulip, and other nicknames we will leave unpublished!), my wonderful wife, who is a great listener and loves me so deeply! Whenever I present a new idea or ambition, you always encourage me to go for it. Our love gets stronger with each passing year—buoyed by the good times and strengthened by adversity! I love you today, tomorrow, and forever!

God, the Creator of Heaven and Earth, from whom all blessings flow, and without whom this book would not have materialized. To God be the glory!

Table of Contents

A Flourishing Dream
Foreword by Peter Merrett

What a distinct pleasure it is to support and celebrate Peter Colwell's wonderful new book. While it is being newly released to the world in 2021, it is indeed a work of art that has in fact been long bubbling away inside Peter's heart and soul for the past fifteen years or so. Now that it has all reached the surface and come alive in the pages that follow, I believe this is actually more than just a book—it is a timely and refreshing tonic for the soul of our world today. More than its printed pages or words, it is a celebration of human spirit, with an inspiring and reassuring message—of hope.

I feel profoundly honored to be the opening voice here, and I am thankful for the serendipitous moments that led to bringing me and Peter together. I have always been fascinated by, and in awe of, the wheels of serendipity. It is one of life's great marvels, and I love the quote by Charlton Heston, who sums it up quite perfectly:

> *Sometimes life drops blessings in your lap without*
> *your lifting a finger. Serendipity, they call it.*

I always liken it to a fortunate accident.

My path first crossed with Peter's in the fall of 2017. I was visiting the United States as the keynote speaker and facilitator at JLL's Mid-Atlantic Property Management Training Conference, which Peter and his colleagues were instrumental in putting together. Yet this moment was an especially memorable treat—witnessing the eager enthusiasm and humble spirit of Peter.

I will never forget the moment as I was closing the general opening session, in the stunning hotel ballroom on the outskirts of Washington, DC. I posed the question to the audience: "Who here is interested in taking their speaking skills to the next level?" Of all the hands that went up amongst the 150 attendees, it was Peter's that went up the fastest! My gift for Peter was an online consultation on how to further develop himself as a speaker. I remember that Peter appeared to practically turn into the character of Charlie Bucket, from Roald Dahl's story of *Charlie and the Chocolate Factory*: He reacted to my gesture as if it was his treasured Golden Ticket! He immediately followed up with me upon my return to Australia, to fix the date to meet.

During our online exchange, I could feel Peter's exuberance literally bursting across the ether. We debated his vision and dream of influencing others, and his desire to guide people on how to become confident leaders. I remember vividly giving Peter two action items, to set his course in motion. Peter promptly implemented both of those steps—and he has been off and running ever since, wildly exceeding my hopes of what he might accomplish within such a short period of time. Within a year of our initial one-hour virtual exchange, Peter had not only joined but had also graduated from the Speaker Academy within the Washington, DC chapter of the National Speakers Association (NSA).

He didn't sit back and wait or put his dream off for a later date. Instead, he invested the time, expense, and effort toward the birth of his new personal vision. As I write this, Peter has just been elected to the Board of Directors of his NSA chapter in Washington, DC. I couldn't be prouder of his eagerness to volunteer for such an important role in serving the speaking industry.

Peter's zest for inspiring others also comes through in his magnificent gift of motivational poetry—a personal delight that he openly admits was something he stumbled upon quite by chance. His abundant love of poetry is amplified by heartfelt personal tales, adventures, and the lessons learned from the friends and colleagues he has encountered on his life's journey. But it is his passion to release his thoughts in such an interesting way that provides his readers with such a potent serving of unquestionable pleasure. Peter has a special way with words that awaken the spirit. There is a rhythm, beat, and heart to his poems, which combine to bring his words alive and deliver special meaning to his readers. To quote one of my favorite excerpts from his poem "Dreams Eventually Flourish":

> *Instead, march ahead to the beat of your drum,*
> *Faithfully following the sweet little hum,*
> *Of a yearning that is burning inside your soul*
> *A feat you must complete to make you whole ...*

I realize that Peter is heartfully practicing his own words and fully living the dream of his life's purpose—bringing a great purity of goodness to the world. The thing I love the most? Seeing him enjoying every single moment of it. His dreams are indeed flourishing, and I can't help but wonder—indeed, what might happen if we all followed suit?

Peter is a family man and comes from a deeply humble upbringing of respectful beliefs. His core is fueled with the warmest authentic enthusiasm, for seeing the best in people. I have every confidence that you will see and feel this in the words ahead.

It is indeed a special privilege to raise the curtain on this gem of a book, and to warmly welcome you to the nourishing marvels that lie in the pages ahead.

So—are you sitting comfortably?

Then let us begin!

Introduction

Have you ever wished you had the confidence and composure to meet life's challenges head on? This book of poetic inspiration and real-life mindset strategies will show you how to invest in your most important asset—your *attitude*!

Following the suggestions in this book will lead to an overflowing sense of hope, confidence, and resilience.

This book is for you if you want to improve your self-regard, create healthier relationships, increase your productivity, and get more satisfaction out of life.

Every example, anecdote, and story in this book is geared toward the refinement of your attitude, with specific action steps you can apply and experiment with immediately. Don't mistake this book for just another "positive thinking" guide. There are plenty of those, and many of them have merit. This book, though, is intended for people who are tired of *saying* they want to improve their lives and are finally ready to *do* whatever it takes to enhance their health and relationships, their finances, and their careers. If you fall into this category, then read on!

To your success,

Peter Colwell

Peter Colwell
September 2021
Germantown, Maryland USA

The Road
to Resilience

by Peter Colwell

Blessed are those who develop the knack
For moving past hardship and sailing right back
No matter how often things get out of whack
Their WILL finds a WAY to get them on track.

What is the secret to others' success,
Helping them forge through the messiest mess?
Bouncing back stronger, surviving the test ...
Learning to THRIVE and bring out their best?

A definite purpose can help us gain ground
Confident that we can turn things around
Leaning on others whose judgment is sound.
Watching our situation abound ...

With nuggets of gold in the form of DESIRE
To finally do what it takes to climb higher
Resolving that nothing will stand in our way
Of reaching the top of the mountain to say:

"Today is my day to soak in the sun!
What nearly got lost was finally won!
Eternal belief in my inner brilliance ...
To navigate the road to resilience!"

chapter one

Choose Your Response to Any Circumstance

... [E]verything can be taken from a man but one thing: the last of the human freedoms—to choose one's attitude in any given set of circumstances, to choose one's own way.

VIKTOR FRANKL

"Mr. Colwell, your blood pressure is 170/100. Are you sure you're feeling OK?" the physician assistant asked.

"Well, I was feeling just fine until you shared that information with me," I replied. "I only came here to check my vitals for a quick physical, so that I could go on a Scout camping trip with my son."

"Let's try the other arm," the PA said, giving me a glimmer of hope that the high reading was a fluke.

"Hmm—it's the same," she revealed. "Why don't you lie down for ten minutes and relax, then I'll come back and take it again."

Ten minutes later: No change.

"I'm afraid your blood pressure is extremely elevated, and we will need to put you on some medication to bring it down," the PA concluded, "especially since you'll be hiking and camping for a week in the mountains."

That moment in the doctor's office, when I was thirty-eight years old, constituted a decision point for me: I could simply start taking the medication as advised, making no other changes in my life; or

I could dig deeper to uncover the root cause(s) of my elevated blood pressure, then figure out a plan to manage this surprise health concern—one often referred to as "the silent killer" because many people aren't aware they're dealing with it, and they therefore fail to seek treatment for it or make the necessary changes to improve it.

I decided to research the causes and effects of high blood pressure. I visited with a cardiologist, got information on the DASH (Dietary Approaches to Stop Hypertension) Diet, and formulated a strategy to take charge of my heart health so that my blood pressure would normalize. I developed a health improvement plan and worked to implement my goals daily, weekly, and monthly.

One additional challenge, though, stood in my way.

Every time I checked my blood pressure, I could feel my heart rate going up—and often my blood pressure went right up with it, especially during visits to the doctor. This had never happened to me before my diagnosis. So in addition to pursuing a healthier lifestyle, I also took on another new mission: overcoming the fear of getting my blood pressure checked.

It was a work-in-progress, but over several months I succeeded, using all the tools at my disposal and eventually reaching a point where I looked forward to checking my blood pressure (especially when I was rewarded with good readings!). Even if the numbers themselves were a bit high sometimes, my fear no longer existed. And erasing this fear emboldened me with the courage to address other fears and concerns in my life.

When I was a child, a dear friend of mine once told me: "Always remember, Peter: mind *over* matter." Situations will rattle us. Life circumstances will upend us. Our best-laid plans will go awry. We will have natural knee-jerk reactions when things go against us. But we *can* ultimately choose our response and approach for the long term—and that will make all the difference in the quality of our lives.

CHOOSE YOUR RESPONSE TO ANY CIRCUMSTANCE

Viktor Frankl, author of *Man's Search for Meaning* and a well-known survivor of the Nazi death camps of Auschwitz and Dachau, called our ability to choose our attitude "the last of the human freedoms." When all else is stripped away from us and our situation is grimmer than grim, we can still leverage our own strength, transcend suffering, and find meaning in our lives. Frankl noted that our "unique opportunity lies in the way in which [we] bear [our] burden."

We can all choose our response to any circumstance in life—a death in the family, a divorce, the break-up of a relationship, a job loss, being snubbed by a friend, or a scary health diagnosis.

Imagine the personal freedom we would experience if we could shift our mindset at any time and make a concerted effort to adopt an improved outlook, one that focuses on solutions instead of dwelling on problems.

Fortunately, we can.

By realizing—and accepting—that we have a choice in how we respond to the burdens and challenges of life, we experience many benefits. We:

- Learn the power of reining in our many thoughts so that we can consider things more clearly and make informed decisions.

- Look at problems, and generate potential solutions, from a more empowered point of view.

- Step back from situations and allow ourselves to be more objective about them.

- Adopt a more resourceful state of mind.

- Avoid saying or doing something we'll regret.

- Get to the real root(s) of problems versus wasting our time, energy, and money on the superficial reason(s).

What *choices* are you making about what you put in your mind? Are you choosing to focus on thoughts of prosperity, or are you instead choosing to stay in a mindset that perpetuates a sense of lacking what you truly desire? Are you choosing to be happy and to seek goodness in others and yourself, or are you choosing to constantly remind yourself of what's wrong with the world and the people in it?

Many of our circumstances, whether pleasant or not, are the result of choices we've made in our lives. Thus, if we want to change our circumstances, we have to choose differently. Specifically, we must choose our behaviors, thought patterns, and perspectives more consciously, purposefully, and wisely.

In short: We need to choose and then develop a can-do attitude—an attitude of intentional flexibility, positivity, willingness to try, determination, and resilience.

Some people are always grumbling because roses have
thorns; I am thankful that thorns have roses.
ALPHONSE KARR

Rescript Your Thoughts

My wife, Trevia, and I used to share a mutual mantra. Although we struggled financially in the early years of our marriage, we realized that our love was strong enough to get us through the lean times. So we would often recite the following phrase: "We are poor, but we have love." We repeated this sentence many times as a sort of buffer for our financial hardships. We thought we were helping ourselves by doing so. Love conquers all, right?

It wasn't until we attended an educational seminar on becoming "financially focused" that we realized we'd been filling our minds with certain beliefs, and that our brains were then manifesting the exact reality we were subconsciously creating.

For a while there, we continued to simply be "poor"—or, rather, underperforming in the financial department—and we continued to "have love." Don't get me wrong: I was grateful my wife and I still had a very loving relationship, but I was not thrilled with the fact that we were still financially challenged. I realized that *we* were responsible for our financial foibles; it wasn't the credit card companies, the banks, or those tempting store advertisements. After all: We had chosen to spend money we didn't have. We were the ones who had been living above our means. We had also been programming our minds to believe that we were "poor," and consequently we kept manifesting that result.

Determined to turn the situation around, we decided to rescript our thoughts. Instead of thinking and saying "we are poor, but we have love," we started to think and say "we are rich *and* we have love"! We even wrote this new mantra on a whiteboard so that we could see it every day.

Within weeks of continually reading and reciting this phrase, we noticed small but steady improvements in our financial situation. We started watching how we spent our money. We looked for bargains and specials to economize wherever possible. We stopped spending money we didn't have. We tightened the reins and kept better track of our income and expenses. We became "financially focused"—the directive of the seminar we had attended.

By making a few simple changes in how we scripted our thoughts and phrased our affirmations, we were better able to make ourselves more conscious of—and smarter about—our spending habits.

Is there a mantra you've been consciously—or perhaps unconsciously—polluting your mind with every day? Do your thoughts need some rescripting? Think about it!

Write down a mantra on the next page
that will get you going and keep you going.

My Mantra

____

____

____

The habit of being happy enables one to be freed, or largely freed, from the domination of outward conditions.
ROBERT LOUIS STEVENSON

Revisit Your Past Choices

Our past choices are excellent predictors of our current situations. Where you are today is the direct or indirect result of a series of decisions you made—and actions you subsequently took—yesterday (and many yesterdays before that), in combination of course with conditions you couldn't foresee.

On the whole, are you proud of the decisions you've made in your life so far? If there are a few regrettable choices in your past, what can you do differently to avoid repeat performances now?

The decisions you've made previously do not have to define your ultimate destiny (unless, of course, you're on the right path; in that case, keep moving forward!). Thinking about some of the critical choices you've made in the past will help you to confidently make important decisions now and in the future. As you build a track record of successfully thinking through the reasons for and against moving in a certain direction, you'll know what signs to look for and strengthen your instincts.

CHOOSE YOUR RESPONSE TO ANY CIRCUMSTANCE

Which choices have been most beneficial for me?

____

____

Which choices have been less than productive for me?

____

____

In which areas of my life today would I like to make different choices?

____

____

What changes am I willing to make?

____

____

Types of Choices

Re-examine Your Current Choices

To make significant and necessary changes in our lives, we also need to assess what choices we are currently making, and then pinpoint areas we need to address.

So ask yourself:

- Who am I investing my valuable time with?
- Which people can I associate with who will bring out the best in me?
- What new skills can I learn about my field of interest?
- What am I doing to advance in my career?
- How can I rearrange my priorities to move in a more positive direction?
- How am I treating my body? What changes, if I were to make them, would be most immediately helpful to me?
- How am I nourishing my mind and spirit? What practices can I implement to be more in tune with myself and more mentally and spiritually healthy?
- What makes me happy and fulfilled?
- What brings me joy?

Periodic self-assessment and reflection on our current life choices helps us make the necessary adjustments we need to get back on track, so that we can live the kind of life we really want.

The greatest revolution of our generation is that of human beings, who, by changing the inner attitudes of their minds, can change the outer aspects of their lives.
MARILYN FERGUSON

*What do your current choices say about you? What can these choices reveal about the person you've become and, more importantly, the person **you wish to become** in the future?*

Build on Your Good Choices

To boost your confidence, remind yourself of the smart choices you've made previously as well as the ones you're making right now. Pinpoint how they have positively influenced your life and then build on that track record of success.

Some of the most rewarding choices I've made personally have been in the areas of education and employment. Ironically, my wisest decisions have involved turning down attractive opportunities for seemingly less-attractive ones. For example, I declined a full academic scholarship to a private high school to get a rigorous education elsewhere. Four years later, I turned down a full academic scholarship to one university so that I could go to a more suitable, more desirable university—one my family and I could only partially pay for. And in yet another instance, right after college, I turned down a high-paying job with benefits to do temporary work with no benefits. In each of these cases, instinct and being true to my values guided my choices.

What life choices—previous and current—are you most proud of? What long-term impact have they had on you?

____

____

____

____

*In the final analysis, it is not what happens that determines
the quality of our lives; it is what we choose to do when
we have struggled to set the sail and then discover,
after all our efforts, that the wind has changed directions. ...
How quickly and responsibly we react to adversity
is far more important than the adversity itself.*
JIM ROHN

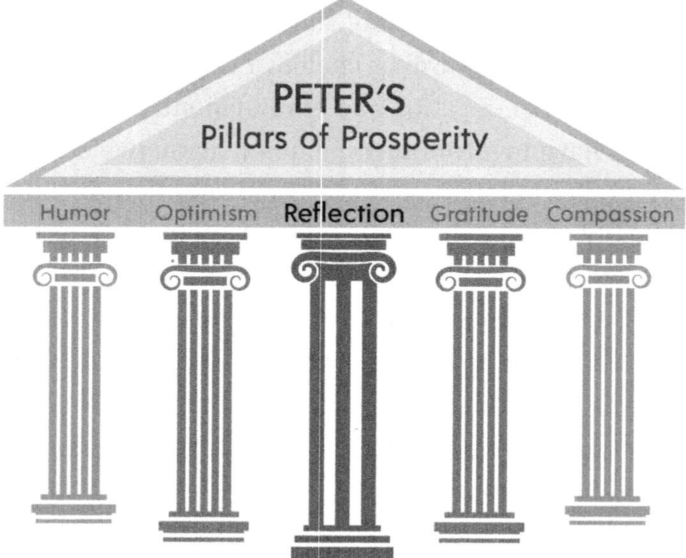

Optimal Life Responses—
Peter's Pillars of Prosperity

If we want to cope with change and adversity—life's downturns—
we must adapt to the moment and choose the most effective
response(s). Unfortunately, though, when we're in the heat of the
moment and all eyes (including our own!) are upon us, we often
have little time to think about what we're doing.

That's why *practicing* is so critical. We can perfect the art of the effective response by practicing it in minor, everyday situations, using a model I call Peter's Pillars of Prosperity.

Each of the pillars is a specific trait or behavior you can call upon to respond effectively to a challenging situation. Think of the pillars as a set of practical, potent ways you can cope with and adapt to various circumstances. Run through each of them in a given circumstance and harness them to regain your footing.

Practice the strategies when the risks are low and you'll be well prepared to use the Pillars of Prosperity when the stakes are high(er) and the pressure is on!

Let's look at each of the pillars in depth.

Pillar #1—Humor

You can and should approach virtually any situation in life in a light-hearted manner. Why? Because a sense of *humor* eases the burden you (and perhaps others) are feeling, softens things up, reduces stress, breaks the tension, and helps us laugh at ourselves.

The use of humor isn't limited to professional comedians or class clowns. In fact, the greatest leaders use humor to connect with people and to earn their cooperation and trust.

You may be thinking: *"Wait a minute! Life can get really complicated, and sometimes there's no place for humor or for a light approach to a heavy subject."* Life situations certainly can get serious. But I've discovered that lightening the load can be our saving grace during especially difficult times. A lightened mood doesn't minimize the severity of the situation; it simply helps us catch our breath and absorb what's happening to and around us.

On September 15, 2001—just four days after the infamous terrorist attacks of September 11th—I was scheduled to be the master of ceremonies for a humorous-speech contest in Washington, DC, just miles from the Pentagon, which had been partially destroyed by a hijacked airliner. Despite the events of that week and the heaviness of the moment, the contest was not rescheduled.

I had prepared plenty of jokes and one-liners for the event. But after September 11th, it seemed awkward, if not downright inappropriate, to laugh and joke about things amidst all the tragedy that had unfolded.

In thinking about how I would approach my task, I decided to break the ice by sharing with the audience a quote I had heard from professional speaker and humorist Ron Culberson: "Life is too important to be taken seriously." This statement reinforced the idea that while life is indeed important, it's also OK to lighten up and enjoy it no matter what's going on around you.

This simple opening thought put people in a frame of mind that it was OK to laugh and let loose for a while.

When we develop the habit of finding and using humor in everyday situations, over time it becomes second nature to us. If you get cut off by a speeding car on the highway, for example, instead of cursing and developing instant road rage, try laughing it off and saying to yourself something like *"she must be late for work"* or *"that guy's had one too many coffees this morning"* or *"he's in the wrong profession—he should be a racecar driver."*

You'll find that there are numerous ways to inject humor into your everyday experiences and defuse tense situations. Here are some specific strategies you can use to lighten things up—for your own sake and that of others around you.

State the Obvious

Sometimes the best way to alleviate tension in a group is to speak directly to the elephant in the room. By plainly stating the obvious, you're bound to get some laughs, as people find relief when someone openly acknowledges an awkward or dicey matter.

One day, I had a crisis in one of the commercial office buildings I used to manage. There was a leak in the electrical room, which could have caused an explosion in the building (water and electricity don't mix too well!). So to ensure the safety of everyone in the five-story complex, I issued an order, with the approval of the building owner, to have the facility completely evacuated.

The building housed military personnel, some of whom were none too pleased that they had to leave the premises. In fact, as afternoon progressed into evening, a couple of the military staff members refused to vacate the building. They were tense and agitated the whole time. They wanted updates from me and my team every twenty to thirty minutes. But due to the nature of the emergency and the need to bring in qualified professionals to assess the situation and discuss potential solutions, we were unable to provide frequent updates. That only increased the tension and made matters worse.

As I walked into the building and waited to be briefed by my building engineer, the two holdout military staffers asked me a bunch of questions I couldn't immediately answer. They also used the crisis to bring up other problems and concerns that had nothing to do with the issue we were dealing with.

"Did you see the door you came in?" one of them asked. "Did you notice that it's still not working? And there's a light out in the parking lot."

I was tempted to yell back: *"What do those issues have to do with the problem we're facing right now?!"*—as I, too, was in the heat of the moment. But I chose instead to reply: "Yes, we have several problems, and we will fix them one at a time." I said it with a smile on my face, thus immediately alleviating the tension in the room. I also admitted that what the military staffers were saying was true, which reduced their resistance.

A lighthearted approach in the moment—combined with honesty—can go a long way toward smoothing over a difficult situation.

Express the Collective Feelings of the Group

One effective way to connect with others and subtly make a point is to express the collective feelings of a group without directly stating what problem it is facing. In doing so, you allow everyone to move on from the experience and to reflect on what's occurred in a more lighthearted way.

I was once asked to be a keynote speaker for a property management summit. The night before my presentation, I spent some time with the group I would be addressing the following day, enjoying a cocktail hour followed by dinner.

Unfortunately, the cooking staff was facing several challenges that evening, which caused a two-hour delay in dinner being served. Just as unfortunately, the restaurant staff failed to provide regular updates about the delay.

The head of the group I'd be speaking to was extremely annoyed and displeased with the long wait, as several attendees had flown in for this annual meeting. But he kept his composure.

Ironically, I had been invited to give a presentation on customer service, of all topics. One of the meeting planners looked over at me during dinner and asked, "Are you going to somehow incorporate this into your presentation tomorrow?"

"Most likely," I smiled.

The next morning, I managed to weave into my presentation—without mentioning it directly—a subtle note about the lack of customer service the evening before. During my speech, I acknowledged the head of the group, thanked him for inviting me to speak, and expressed my appreciation for his calm demeanor and patience during the "situation" that had occurred the previous night.

Most people had chosen not to mention the snafu, so I decided to bring it up quickly, take a lighthearted approach to it, and move on. The result? Everyone erupted in quick laughter.

Use the Power of Understatement (a.k.a. Subtlety)

Another way to lighten people's moods—and/or defuse a tense or stressful situation—is to be subtle in your approach and make a significant understatement. Instead of stating just how painful or difficult a situation is/was, *underplay it for effect.* Doing so will likely generate laughter and "let the air out of the balloon."

Imagine yourself, for instance, as part of a group of hikers that had a brush with disaster earlier in the day—a situation where you all nearly slid down the mountain or almost got struck by lightning. Experiences like these can be traumatic, especially if you dwell on the fear you felt and the severity of what might have resulted.

If you're helping the group debrief afterwards, instead of saying "that hike was dangerous and scary," you could say "that hike was a tad treacherous, wasn't it."

"Just a tad!" will be the inevitable response from the group, followed by laughter—and maybe a few sighs of relief!

We all experience close calls that remind us how fragile and precious life is. A well-delivered understatement—inserted into the conversation when tension is at its highest—is akin to releasing a valve to reduce water pressure to a lower, more functional level. It calms you and everyone else down, helps you all think more clearly, and allows everyone to make better decisions and maintain perspective.

Lift Somber Moments

I'll never forget when I was unexpectedly called—in the moment—to be a pallbearer at the funeral for the father of one of my former assistant managers.

I didn't know any other members of the family, so I had just been standing in the back row of the church. Suddenly, the family needed someone to fill in as a pallbearer, so I obliged.

My assistant must have seen the nervous look on my face as I was assuming this task during a very somber moment. She looked over at me and shouted: "If you drop my daddy, I'm not coming into work on Tuesday!" There were smiles and laughter all around, giving everyone a much-needed break from their grieving.

In another instance, just a few weeks after my wife and I had lost a loved one ourselves, the grief we were experiencing was still quite fresh. We were in a bit of a daze, and we weren't feeling the holiday spirit that most everyone else was feeling, despite the festive decorations and music that surrounded us in the store where we were shopping.

We managed to snap out of the doldrums temporarily, though, when we each instinctively grabbed long rolls of wrapping paper, turned them into makeshift "lightsabers," and acted out a famous scene from *The Empire Strikes Back*—*"[Luke], I am your father!"*—right there in the store aisle. It was a moment of levity that gave us a much-needed lift from the weight of the very real pain we were going through.

If we can laugh a bit even at funerals and in other difficult situations, then we can rely on humor to get us through virtually any challenge we are facing.

Think of a challenge you're going through right now. How can a bit of humor ease the situation?

____

____

____

Pillar #2—Optimism

*No problem can be solved from the same level
of consciousness that created it.*

ALBERT EINSTEIN

One of the most vital tools we can carry with us throughout our lives is unyielding *optimism*—an unwavering hope that things will turn out for the best. Optimism is a philosophy of living that helps us see through the darkness of the moment and envision the brightness of the future. It allows us to navigate through negative experiences and come out of them stronger, happier, and wiser.

Ever since I was a little boy, I've been determined to remain "one of the optimistic ones." I was always a believer, not a doubter. I had faith I would overcome any challenge or obstacle that life threw my way.

Luckily, I've never outgrown this mindset. As an adult, I'm still a firm believer in the power of an optimistic attitude. Time and again, I have watched how optimism helps people prevail through even the most difficult of circumstances.

In the summer of 2020, my mom—Marjorie Virginia Colwell—was diagnosed with late-stage pancreatic cancer at the age of eighty-one. The doctors gave our family grim news: that my mom's cancer was terminal, and that she had just a matter of months to live.

Despite this difficult prognosis, Mom dug in her heels and remained optimistic. She followed all medical orders, adjusted her diet as needed, and ultimately decided to pursue chemotherapy that could give her a fighting chance (albeit an outside one) of defeating the tumor.

When her oncologist told us there was a "ray of hope" that he could shrink the tumor if my mom responded well to the chemotherapy treatments, Mom decided to give it a chance. Her optimism was unrelenting, and she was determined to keep a smile on her face and to bravely meet the demands of each day.

That hopeful conversation with the oncologist spurred me to write a poem:

A RAY OF HOPE

by Peter Colwell

From a distance—shining through—arrives a ray of hope ...
Often just as life has pulled us down a slippery slope
Precisely timed to lift our mood and elevate awareness
Hope can counter desperate times and build a sense of fairness.

Unexpected pleasant news can be a welcome stranger
Sparking new, exciting thoughts that steer us far from danger
Grabbing hold of goodness, in all its splendid glory
Gives us **MOTIVATION** to redefine our story.

Hopeful words retold each day will fuel us to the finish
Giving birth to joyfulness that no one can diminish!
Strength of body, mind, and soul are goals we can achieve ...
By living faithfully today, determined to **BELIEVE**!

While my mom's chemotherapy initially appeared to be working, and she had some good days to enjoy precious time with her family, the treatments ultimately did her more harm than good. On the fiftieth anniversary of my parents' meeting, Mom's health took a turn for the worse, and two days later she moved into hospice care from the comfort of her home.

Two weeks after that—with my dad, my sister, and me by her bedside—my mom peacefully passed away. Before she died, she made sure to tell us "I feel loved" and "I'm ready to go." The optimistic spirit my mom exuded throughout her life is a gift she has passed down to her children and grandchildren.

Optimism doesn't ensure a perfect result or the best outcome, of course. But it does help us stay fully engaged in finding solutions and minimizing the emotional impact of problems, regardless of how things ultimately turn out.

A Push to the Finish

In 1999, my wife (then fiancée), Trevia, and I ran the Marine Corps Marathon together in Washington, DC. Trevia had been inspired watching me run the same marathon the year before; she'd even told me at the finish line that she wanted to train and participate with me the next year.

So the following spring, we signed up for the race (and raised funds to fight leukemia while we were at it). Then, over the next six months, we trained together in warm, cool, rainy, and very hot weather. By race day, we felt we had adequately prepared, physically and mentally, for the big event.

But at approximately mile twenty-three (i.e., with just three miles to go), Trevia started to feel agonizing pain in her lower back. It was overwhelming, and it began to slow her down, almost to the point of her dropping out of the race. Knowing she needed some words of optimism, I came alongside her and shouted: "I believe in you! You've come this far, and even if we need to slow down for a bit we can finish this together!"

The hopeful (and sincerely felt) words—combined with lots of water and Gatorade—became her fuel down the homestretch. We crossed the finish line hand in hand. She even beat me by a second!

Think of a challenge you're going through right now. How can a healthy dose of optimism see you through it?

____

____

[B]e so strong that nothing can disturb your peace of mind.
CHRISTIAN LARSON, FROM "THE OPTIMIST'S CREED"

Pillar #3—Gratitude

*Some people could be given an entire field of roses and only
see the thorns in it. Others could be given a single weed and
only see the wildflower in it. Perception is a key component
to gratitude. And gratitude a key component to joy.*
AMY WEATHERLY

None of us is immune to adversity. Monetary wealth won't shelter us from hardship. Fame won't keep us from experiencing heartache. Material possessions won't excuse us from difficulties. Every one of us will face challenges throughout our lifetimes. Adversity, in many ways, can be a blessing by helping us deepen—and harness—our sense of *gratitude*.

Our son, Petey, was born with a heart murmur, discovered on Mother's Day—when he was just one day old. At three days of age, Petey was diagnosed with a *Ventricular Septal Defect* (VSD): a hole in the wall (*septum*) that separates the heart's lower chambers (*ventricles*), allowing blood to pass from the left to the right side of the heart. The oxygen-rich blood then gets pumped back to the lungs instead of out to the body, causing the heart to work harder.

We were told this condition would need to be fixed surgically, but not immediately. Three weeks later, however, we had to rush Petey to the emergency room of Children's Hospital in Washington, DC, as he was unable to keep his food down. He would spend the next ten hours in the ER.

Eventually, the team of physicians involved in Petey's care told us that our newborn would have to undergo surgery to repair a tightening in his stomach known as *Pyloric Stenosis*, which occurs most commonly in first-born males in the first few weeks of life. Petey spent the next week in the hospital, recovering from the surgery. (His parents were also recovering emotionally!)

Thinking we were out of the woods, Trevia and I returned home to try to restore a sense of normalcy (or, perhaps, new normalcy) to our lives as new parents. After a visit with a cardiologist the next week to follow up on Petey's heart issue, we were informed that our son had a congenital heart defect known as *tetralogy of Fallot*—a complex medical problem with four areas of concern: 1) the VSD discovered when Petey was three days old; 2) narrowing of the pulmonary valve; 3) thickening of the muscle of the right ventricle; and 4) an overriding (displaced) aorta. Petey would have to undergo open-heart surgery to resolve these significant cardiac issues.

As English historian Thomas Fuller once said: "We never know the worth of water till the well is dry." Petey's heart and stomach conditions—at such an early age, no less—helped me and my wife appreciate the value of life itself, and to be grateful for every moment we had with our newborn son, none of which we took for granted.

At three months of age, Petey underwent open-heart surgery to repair his congenital heart condition. The procedure lasted four hours. Thanks to the prayers of many people and the refined skill of his surgeon, Petey recovered quickly and was able to come home six days after surgery.

We followed up with his cardiologist regularly. When Petey was nearly two and a half years old, I took him in for his routine, scheduled exam. After the test results came back, the cardiologist walked into the room with a grim look on his face.

"Mr. Colwell," he said, "I'm sorry to inform you that we found an obstruction in your son's heart. He will need to have another surgery to fix it."

As difficult as this news was for *me* to bear, my heart ached when I thought about having to share it with Trevia. I headed straight to the school where she was teaching—only to get flagged on the way by a police officer. Apparently, I had been driving eleven miles over the speed limit.

"License and registration, please," said the officer.

I reached over for my vehicle registration and immediately burst into tears.

The sight of a grown man crying took the officer by surprise. He asked what was wrong. I told him through my sobs that my son needed to have a second open-heart surgery, and that I was on my way to tell my wife.

The officer handed my registration back to me and said: "Here. I just want you to get there in one piece."

A few minutes later, I broke the news to Trevia. We cried and hugged several times, then regrouped and prepared for next steps.

The following month, Petey underwent his second heart surgery. The procedure was supposed to last four hours. About two hours in, the surgeon came into the waiting room with his gloves off, which caused us some concern.

But the news was good.

"The surgery is all done and went quicker than expected," the surgeon said. "Your son is breathing on his own and is doing quite well!"

Music to our ears!

The adversity we faced at that time was overwhelming and scary. But we ultimately decided to view our situation as a chance to deepen our faith in a positive outcome, to become more knowledgeable about congenital heart disease, and to learn how to support each other during the ordeal.

As I write this, Petey is now an eighteen-year-old young man heading off to college. He hasn't needed any additional heart surgeries, though he continues to be monitored yearly. Gratitude abounds every time we leave the cardiologist's office with a clean bill of health.

Petey's original cardiologist—the person who detected Petey's condition and then oversaw its treatment—retired just a few years ago, when Petey was fourteen. Petey wrote him a special note, wishing him a happy retirement and thanking him for saving his life!

Think of a challenge you're going through right now. How can choosing an attitude of gratitude make a positive difference?

____

____

____

____

Pillar #4—Compassion

Our ability to show *compassion*—to ourselves and to others—will serve us well when we find ourselves somehow dealing with difficulties and misfortune.

When things go wrong—and they will—it's incredibly easy to simply turn inward and complain about the unfairness of it all. We can wallow in a "why me?" mentality and blame other people and circumstances for putting us in a tough spot.

Or we can choose to soften our approach and give ourselves (and others) a little dose of lovingkindness. Instead of beating ourselves up over our mistakes and struggles, we can acknowledge the fact that we all stumble and fall once in a while, and that difficulties are very much a part of the human condition.

A Community of Compassionate Kindness

When my daughter, Vanessa, was approaching three, she was hit by a car while she was playing with her big brother, Petey, and some friends in our neighborhood. The accident left her with a fractured right leg.

Yet amidst all the chaos and scariness of the moment, we were graced and surrounded by compassionate kindness.

The driver who hit Vanessa, apologizing profusely, handed me a first-aid kit and attempted to stop Vanessa's bleeding. Our next-door neighbor came out with towels. A twelve-year-old girl called 911, since I was suffering from laryngitis and had my hands full with first aid. Then Petey, age seven at the time, came up to me and asked calmly: "Daddy, what can I do to help?" So I gave him my cell phone and told him to call Mommy to let her know what had happened.

Before long, an ambulance arrived to transport Vanessa to the hospital. Another neighbor stood next to me and gave me a shoulder to cry on.

Vanessa underwent emergency surgery that night, and her leg was placed in a hot-pink cast. Within three months, she was fully healed.

But the emotional recovery for Trevia and me took a bit longer. Nearly losing a child to an accident is a moment that gets replayed over and over in the minds of parents—and it was no different for us. We kept wondering how the situation could have played out differently so that Vanessa could have avoided the experience. And yet we also realized that the outcome could have been a whole lot worse.

What really helped me move past the incident—and stop rehashing it in my mind—was when a good friend of mine said to me: "You know, Peter, it's not your fault. This could have happened to anyone. Accidents happen every day. And everything turned out well in the end. You have a lot to be grateful for." Those powerful words helped me turn the corner and take a big, thankful sigh of relief about the fortunate outcome of an unfortunate circumstance.

There are events in our lives that we cannot foresee or avoid. When these painful events occur, we need to be kind to ourselves and let ourselves off the hook.

A compassionate reminder of our essential goodness, from people who know us and trust us, sure helps too!

Holding On and Letting Go

When you look into your mother's eyes, you know
that is the purest love you can find on this earth.

MITCH ALBOM

I've had many chances in my life—most recently during the last four months of her life in 2020, when she battled pancreatic cancer—to look into my mother's eyes, feel her love, and know I was always in the presence of God when I was with her.

My mom always made me feel loved and special. She instilled in me a belief in myself that helped me overcome self-doubt when life would throw its inevitable curveballs.

Determined to raise a self-reliant son (and daughter, for that matter), Mom sent me (and my sister!) off to summer camp at a very early age. I clearly recall stepping, at the tender age of six, onto a school bus in Central Square in East Boston and waving goodbye to my parents as I headed off to East Boston Summer Camps for two weeks.

While I initially had no qualms, not knowing what I was getting myself into, I spent the first two days at camp crying my eyes out; I wanted to go home. I sent a postcard the first day, asking if my parents could pick me up. I got to make one phone call to my mom to ask her to come get me. Her response: "Give [camp] a try. In a couple of days, you'll probably start having a lot of fun."

She was right.

After a while, I started to enjoy myself. And by the end of the two weeks, I was actually sad to leave my fellow campers.

That time at summer camp instilled in me a love of the outdoors that only grew as the years passed. I attended Christian camps, music camps, basketball camps, and many Boy Scout adventures.

When I was fourteen, I told my parents I wanted to attend the National Scout Jamboree in Virginia. But they said they couldn't afford it; it wasn't in their budget.

They saw my passion for Scouting grow as I moved toward the rank of Eagle Scout. So the next year, I asked them if I could go to the World Scout Jamboree—a gathering of twenty thousand Scouts from 120 countries around the world. The jamboree was about five times as expensive as the National Jamboree in Virginia had been the previous year, and it was to be held at Seoraksan National Park in South Korea. But to my surprise, Mom said: "You're in! We will figure out a way to pay for it!"

So on an August morning in 1991, several close family members gathered and said farewell to me at Logan International Airport in Boston as I took off on a journey to the other side of the globe—my first time on an airplane. It was the experience of a lifetime! I remember talking to Mom and Dad for about sixty seconds on a quick international call and sharing the extraordinary adventures I was having: eating kimchi for the first time, making friends from several countries, trying out athletic events to test my endurance. I could feel the enthusiasm and exuberance coming from Mom's (and Dad's) voice. It was yet another example of her instilling confidence in me and helping me become a self-reliant, capable human being.

And yet, the push to raise self-reliant children by no means diminished Mom's deep and abiding love for us, nor her yearning for connection with us.

In August 1993, I went away to college, beginning my freshman year at Georgetown University in Washington, DC. A few months later, during Thanksgiving break, I discovered that my mom had missed me so much during the few months I'd been gone that she'd developed a "nighttime ritual" of saying good night to me (as if I were there) and kissing the pillow on the bed where I used to lay. It was her way of holding on while still letting go.

It would not be until much later in my life, when I had children of my own, that I would fully comprehend and appreciate the power of my mom's emotions at that time—the utter depth of her love and commitment.

Today, as a parent of two teenagers, it's very clear to me how abundant my mom's love was (and has always remained) through-out my life. I now find myself in the "sandwich generation," trying to gently let go of my own children while still holding them close, and at the same time faced with a new reality where I must let go of the earthly connections I had with my mom—the hugs, the kisses, the walks, the talks, the late-night heart-to-hearts—and hold on fervently to heavenly ways to connect with her. Holding on while letting go ...

My mom's love will never end. It will live on in the hearts and minds of all who knew and cared about her. Her energy lit up a room and imprinted on people what families are all about: enthu-siastic love and compassion for each other.

That compassion showed up even in the final hours of Mom's life, when she looked at my dad, my sister, and me and said: "I'm sorry I haven't smiled much lately"—then gave us the biggest grin. Just what we needed! Right up through her very last moments of life, she was thinking of others.

Are you struggling with the balance of holding on to someone you love while still giving them room to grow (or move on)? Goodbyes are never easy. But they are a necessary part of life. The pain of any adjustment period is temporary. Love is eternal.

THE MAGIC OF EMPATHY

by Peter Colwell

Look into another's eyes and you'll begin to realize
The magic that occurs when we can take the time to empathize.
Our deepest truth can't be concealed.
Real emotions get revealed.

Our eyes display an inner knowing
A heart in pain ... or a soul that's glowing
A mind that's stretched and bound to break
A soul that's stirring ... about to wake

Darkness often turns to light
When others join us in our plight
Turning weakness into might
Giving us the will to fight

Another day, another hour
Empathy can give us power
To lift ourselves above the fray
Knowing we can **WIN THE DAY**!

Think of a challenge you're going through right now. How can com-passion—for yourself and/or others—improve your situation?

____

____

____

Pillar #5—Reflection

The central Pillar of Prosperity is *reflection*—the act of looking inward, being still, and contemplating in calmness what is going on around you.

The other four Pillars of Prosperity refer to what we say (either to ourselves or to others) and how we say it. Reflection is the pause between stimulus and response—or the pause after the initial, knee-jerk response—and it can range from a few minutes to a much longer period of time when possible.

The practice of reflection allows us to search our soul for answers—answers that may sometimes be readily apparent, but that more often require some digging to reveal themselves. Often, the solutions to difficult problems and decisions will emerge when we give ourselves uninterrupted time to clear our mind and listen to our inner voice.

I once made the difficult choice—after much reflection—to part ways with an employer, knowing in my heart of hearts that it was the right thing for me to do. I confided in a close friend about my decision. He replied:

"Well done. Wisely done. You have chosen yourself today— and that will be good for you AND your family (especially your kids). They will see a guy walking his talk, even when it's damn hard. The guy doing that talk-walking will see himself doing so when he looks in the mirror. I just want to express my respect and admiration for the tough choice you've made."

If we don't reflect, we won't have the calmness and clarity to make tough, complicated decisions. If, on the other hand, we intentionally add the practice of reflection to our daily toolkit, we will be armed with a proven strategy that will help us whenever life gets overwhelming or big decisions are on the horizon.

Reflection Builds Resilience

My good friend Michael K. Jackson (the other Michael Jackson, as he often says!) is an inspirational speaker who shares personal life lessons on how to overcome setbacks and rise above challenges.

Mike has created a resilience-building blueprint that he developed after the tragic loss of his father during Hurricane Maria, a deadly Category 5 storm that devastated Dominica, St. Croix, and Puerto Rico in September 2017 and ranks as the third-costliest tropical cyclone on record.

It was during his grieving process that Mike reflected not only on the loss of his dad, but on all the losses and all the adversity he'd faced up to that point in his life. He ultimately recognized that a pattern had emerged—a particular way he handled stress—and thus his plan of action was born. He implemented a hurricane-proof (pun intended) blueprint to overcoming stress. Two of the components are: *meditation* and *notating his mind state* (i.e., journaling).

Meditation

Meditation has always been a crucial practice in Mike's life. The reflective, mind-clearing habits of meditation center and still him regardless of what's swirling around him—challenges that come from left and right and all over the place. When in doubt, he puts his hands together, closes his eyes, and goes straight to prayer: a dialogue with his Creator.

As long as God allows Mike to wake up in the morning, he says, he feels thankful. Mike knows that it's easy to become complacent and to discount our blessings. But there are many of them, if we are willing to bring them to light. If we are still breathing, we still have hope.

Don't discount your blessings.
MICHAEL K. JACKSON

Notating the Mind State

Research shows that journaling—reflection in written form—has many of the same positive effects that meditation does when it comes to reducing your stress and boosting your well-being.

For starters, journaling allows us to look back on old entries and realize that what we thought was perhaps a life-changing or life-ending circumstance in fact made us stronger. This realization gives us hope in the present: If we survived a previous ordeal and we're still here, then we can certainly get through the ordeal we're facing now.

Wellness coach Elizabeth Scott—in her VeryWellMind.com article entitled "The Benefits of Journaling for Stress Management"—points out that journaling offers a host of other benefits as well:

- It helps us clarify our thoughts and feelings.
- It gives us a practical tool we can use to "hash out" problems.
- It helps us process events in our lives, particularly those involving trauma.
- It improves our cognitive functioning.
- It even strengthens our immune system.

While journaling may seem like yet another task to add to your to-do list, there are some easy ways to get into the journaling habit. Thanks to modern technology, there are numerous journaling apps available for mobile devices. You can type your journal entry in, record your voice, talk to text, take pictures, and record emotions with emojis or quick phrases.

Mike has been journaling for twenty years now. He began when he was going through some major financial and relationship problems. Before that, he says, he'd thought journaling was solely for teenage girls! So he was reluctant to get out a pen and pad and start writing. But once he did, journaling proved to be a cathartic activity that has helped him heal and move past hardships—and on to better things.

Beyond being just a reflective practice, journaling can be a refreshing practice as well. The progress we make in what we think and how we feel as we're journaling can provide a surge of much-needed hope that we can harness to ride out our current challenges.

Think of a challenge you're going through right now. How can routine written reflection set you on a better course?

____

____

____

____

BACK ON YOUR FEET

by Peter Colwell

Shot from a cannon
Afloat in the air
Uncertain of what looms ahead

Lie the dreams and desires
Found spinning like spires ...
A spool of unraveling thread

We must remain agile
When emotions get fragile
So thoughts can get fully expressed

Internal discovery brings
solid recovery
When the root of the matter's addressed.

What a wonderful feeling to finally land
securely on both of our feet!

Satisfied knowing
We'll never stop growing
Until our life journey's complete!

3

KEY TAKEAWAYS
from Chapter One

1. We are going to experience highs and lows. It's how we respond to them that helps us move forward.

2. Practice Peter's Pillars of Prosperity when the stakes are low so that you'll be ready to use them effectively when the stakes are high.

3. Journaling can be a game changer that improves our outlook and even our physical health.

The Little Things

by Peter Colwell

When pressures mount and stress takes hold
When chaos looms and prospects fold
We might lose sight of dreams of old
And lose our will to break the mold.

But to our rescue each day brings
A secret joy called "little things."
An unexpected twist of fate
A flood of favor at our gate

Words of hope that build desire
Even though the threat be dire
Love to nudge us up the spire
Rekindling our inner fire

A hug and kiss from those we love
A gentle message from above
Reminding us to persevere
To move ahead in spite of fear

The pillars of prosperity
Are grounded in temerity
A bold belief that nature brings
A treasure known as "little things."

chapter two

Take Action to Shape Your Life's Direction

*We all make mistakes, have struggles, and even regret
things in our past. But you are not your mistakes,
you are not your struggles, and you are here now
with the power to shape your day and your future.*
STEVE MARABOLI

"Write your goals down … in pencil." "Be true to yourself." "Stand up
for yourself." As I sat under a big white tent on a scorching Saturday
in May, preparing to watch my wife receive her master's degree from
Hood College, I was mesmerized by the commencement address.

The featured speaker was Lisa Myers, the veteran political cor-
respondent for NBC News. She opened by congratulating the graduates and telling them she'd be offering them advice for navigating
through the next chapters in their lives.

While many people might not remember who their high school
or college commencement speaker was, or what they had to say for
that matter, Myers delivered a challenging, inspiring message that
was impossible to forget—a message of embracing new beginnings
with passion and enthusiasm. She talked about the importance of
combining purposeful planning with flexible living. She urged us all
to use our conscience as our compass and to welcome challenges
and opportunities in our lives.

Her message inspired me to think about my future, and to re-examine my personal and professional goals. That's something we *all* need to do, at least periodically, so that our vision of our life's direction remains fresh and vital to us—and we continue to take inspired actions each day toward what we truly want in life.

AWAKEN TO A NEW DAY

by Peter Colwell

The promise of a new beginning greets us early in the morn'
Our hopes start rising with the sun ...
A brand-new day is born!

A glimmer then a glowing light
Emerging right before our sight
Rising up with awe and might
Another chance to get it right!

Set your sights on greater things
Trusting that the future brings
Delights beyond what you'd expect
Allowing dreams to resurrect.

Spirits lifted now can soar
Letting out a mighty ROAR!
Calling you to be your best
Urging you to live with ZEST!

Another Chance to Get It Right

Life is filled with opportunities for new beginnings. Taking advantage of these opportunities requires a positive attitude along with the willingness to make some clear, definitive changes—to take inspired action.

Every day can be a new beginning for you. As you work toward meeting the demands of your job and career, your family life, and your social and community obligations, you have the opportunity—through the mastery of your attitude—to make each day better than the last.

Chances are you're going through *some* sort of transition in your personal or professional life right now. Maybe you're unemployed and looking for work. Perhaps you're between relationships. Maybe you're adjusting to being a first-time parent, entering a new line of work, becoming an empty nester, or living in a new home.

Transition is one of the most common stress-inducing situations. Marriage, divorce, relocating, getting fired from a job, starting a new one: These transitions are all difficult. But they also represent new beginnings—and new chances to soar.

The world is round, and the place which may seem
like the end may also be only the beginning.
IVY BAKER PRIEST

GET READY FOR AN UPSWING
by Peter Colwell

Get ready for life to turn things around.
Dreams that were lost will finally be found!
Hopes once diminished will reappear
If you take fruitful action in spite of your fear.

Positive thoughts and persistent action
Set into motion a chain reaction.
Offering us an invitation
To live our lives with inspiration!

The secret of success is ENTHUSIASM
Helping us to cross any chasm.
Bridging the gap from A to Z
Lighting the way to our destiny!

Say to yourself: "I'm well equipped.
I'll do what it takes to flip the script.
I'm so very close to reaching the summit.
Now's not the time to let my dreams plummet."

"Joy is my path. With faith I can sing.
I am truly ready for an upswing!"

The "Move!" Mindset

When you're going through a transition, be it a health challenge, financial worries, or a career crisis, the one thing that can pull you through it is your mindset—the way you choose to view what's happening to you and why. We can't control what other people say or do, or how they will act or react, but we can choose our mindset.

A positive, action-oriented mindset will help you weather life's storms and surprises. Resiliency and flexibility will help you see past the pressures of the moment to the beauty of what lies ahead. A hopeful heart will set you up for greater success and enjoyment in life.

Conversely, a negative and limiting mindset will leave you prone to worry, fear, and anxiety. And a rigid mindset will expose you only to the downsides of things, putting you at risk of near-constant frustration.

Which results would you prefer?

One lesson I learned many years ago, from watching (and playing) a video game with my son, Petey, is that when life knocks you down, you need to get back up and *keep moving.*

The object of Mario Kart is to race through several courses and overcome obstacles along the way. On the road to the finish line, the game's characters get ink thrown in their faces, get zapped by lightning, get stomped on, get bumped off the road, get shrunken down, get spun around, and occasionally get flattened like a pancake!

The key to winning what appears to be a very frustrating game is to not allow any of the outward conditions to distract you. If you get inked, for example, you need to shake it off and keep moving. When you get stomped on, bumped, and spun around, you need to redirect yourself and keep moving.

To reach your goals and live your dreams, you need to develop a laser-like focus on your objectives, stay calm amidst the chaos around you, get in sync with the ebb and flow of life—and keep moving! You'll run into delays and difficulties, just like everyone else does. Keep moving! With patient and persistent movement, many of your goals will come to fruition.

Avoid "Comfortable Captivity"

Many people avoid moving in their lives, whatever form it takes, because they fear—perhaps dread—the inevitable stress that their actions might cause. But if, for example, you stay in a job or a relationship that no longer fulfills you, you will experience something even worse than stress.

I call it "comfortable captivity."

When you're in comfortable captivity, your creativity, initiative, and potential are held hostage by limitations imposed upon you by others—or by you yourself. You're forced to suppress your ideas, your knowledge, and your leadership ability. Comfortable captivity may show up in the form of an invisible ceiling preventing you from moving up in your organization, or numerous hurdles placed in your path to promotion and advancement.

I have presented to many groups of administrative professionals, secretaries, executive assistants, and other office support personnel who face this sort of challenge quite frequently. On the one hand, they can become very proficient in their supporting roles. But on the other, their superb skill all too often leads to a feeling of comfort in their roles. Over time, this comfort leads to stagnation and the stifling of their career growth.

Ironically, this stifling emerges because the support professionals' expert abilities are either taken for granted by upper management or, worse, are so valued by senior executives that the support professionals get pigeonholed into permanent positions—management's attempt to hold on to good employees. This phenomenon may lead to higher salaries or more perks in the short term. But in the long run, the result can be detrimental to the employees who want to accelerate their careers.

Fear of the unknown prevents most of us from exploring what our lives *could* be like. Instead, we stick with the familiar. No surprises. No sudden changes. No leaps of faith. Many people, for example, would rather stay in a miserable relationship than risk being alone or having to look for someone else to spend their time with.

When we get too comfortable with the familiar and shy away from opportunities to take a risk or make a big change in our lives, we wind up in what I call "holding patterns." Some examples:

- Staying in a job that no longer challenges you.
- Remaining in a friendship that no longer fulfills you (or the other person).
- Avoiding opportunities for travel, promotion, or advancement.
- Procrastinating the completion of an important project.
- Holding on to possessions you no longer need.

- Identifying strongly with negative thoughts and self-defeating beliefs.

You can beat comfortable captivity, though; you can break free of holding patterns. You can come alive inside with enthusiasm and a renewed sense of purpose.

If you're tired of the same old routine at work, for instance—if you need more intellectual, emotional, or social stimulation—discuss your needs with your boss or supervisor. If you're your own boss (i.e., self-employed), consider outsourcing the least interesting aspects of your business to make time and room in your life for the more enjoyable and career-enhancing tasks.

Opportunities for personal and professional growth are abundant if you're willing to look for them—and then take action. So instead of making excuses for staying in your comfortable holding pattern, branch out and try something new. Take a class. Learn a skill or refine one you already have. Instead of overanalyzing the pros and cons of a new opportunity, take a solid step forward by signing up for that course or workshop, realizing you're making a direct and worthwhile investment—in yourself!

Integrate Self-Discipline into Your Life

Without self-discipline, your life will be a series of broken promises—most of them promises made to, and broken by, yourself. You may be able to live that way for a while. But eventually, your lack of self-discipline will spill over into virtually every area of your life, ultimately affecting the people around you too.

Suppose, for example, that you promise to meet someone new at a specific time and place. The other person is counting on you to keep your word. They arrive at the predetermined meeting place and wait an hour for you to show—but you don't, so they have no choice but to leave.

This is a terrible first impression to make. The other person may well automatically assume some less than positive things about you, not even having met you:

- *"This person can't keep commitments."*
- *"This person doesn't respect and value my time."*
- *"This person is unreliable and irresponsible."*

Whether these conclusions are true or not, it's difficult to erase them—because it's always tough to overcome a negative impression we've left on someone due to our undisciplined behavior.

If we *are* self-disciplined, on the other hand, we are far more likely to keep our promises—to others and to ourselves—and to truly commit to the action(s) necessary to maximize the highs and manage the lows of life.

Let's look at a few ways you can practice aligning your actions with your words—and improve your relationships (with others and yourself) at the same time.

> *If your actions don't live up to your words,*
> *you have nothing to say.*
> DASHANNE STOKES

Make Small Promises to Yourself—and Keep Them

One effective way to develop your self-discipline is to make small promises to yourself—and then *honor them*. Some examples:

- Waking up when your alarm goes off instead of hitting the snooze button.
- Taking an early-morning run when you say you're going to.
- Meeting deadlines you set for yourself.

Once you master the art of keeping simple promises to yourself, you can move on to more consequential ones like tackling your finances, starting an investment portfolio, or pursuing a new degree or studying a specialty in your field of interest.

Making, and then keeping, promises to yourself boosts your self-respect. It helps you believe (rightly!) that you will follow through on your commitments. And before long, others will begin to respect and admire you for your committed attitude and actions.

A disciplined mind is absolutely
necessary for sustained success.
PETER COLWELL

Take Little Steps Each Day

One reason so many people fail to sustain success for the long term is that they get all fired up about a new project, then run out of steam shortly thereafter.

The key to keeping your momentum is to consistently incorporate discipline into your life on the little things, doing a bit each day and letting the results accumulate over time.

Recently, I came across an article by Robert G. Allen, author of *Nothing Down* and co-author (with Mark Victor Hansen) of *The One-Minute Millionaire*. Allen's article discusses simplifying your way to achievement, and in it he recommends taking small, consistent steps each day to realize enormous success.

Allen has applied this principle to his work in real estate, publishing, and several other disciplines, with much success. You can do the same; you can use this approach in practically any area of your life and progress slowly but surely toward your goals. For example:

- If you'd like to lose weight, commit yourself to thirty minutes a day on the treadmill (or whichever form of exercise you choose).

- If you want to write a book, begin by writing one page a day, or even just two paragraphs a day if you're really pressed for time.

- If you need meditation and silence, schedule it—block off a specific amount of time each day to find some inner peace.

Small investments of self-disciplined time and effort really do add up, often to dramatic, positive changes to both your attitude and your well-being.

Itemize Your Bad Habits and Work on Them One by One

An excellent exercise for building a more self-disciplined life is to make a list of your bad habits and then work to eliminate them, one at a time.

Biting your nails, overeating, and smoking are common bad habits. Others include excessive exposure to television or the computer/phone, cutting people off during conversations, and not picking up after yourself. (I've been guilty of a few of these. Just ask my wife!)

Trying to eliminate all our bad habits at once is usually counterintuitive and overwhelming, and therefore ineffective. Focusing on one concern at a time, on the other hand, helps us methodically build confidence in our ability to eradicate bad habits from our lives—by once again leveraging the power of cumulative self-discipline.

In his bestselling book *The Greatest Salesman in the World*, author Og Mandino notes that "only a habit can subdue another habit." So to eliminate your *bad* habits, you must replace them with *good* habits. For example, if you're struggling with punctuality, work on developing the habit of arriving early for appointments and meetings. If you're struggling to get up early in the morning, experiment with setting your alarm a half-hour early. If you can't seem to get away from the apps on your mobile device, try implementing a "no phone policy" one day a week or during certain hours of the day.

Good habits are the key to all success.
Bad habits are the unlocked door to failure.
OG MANDINO

"Don't Hit the Delete Button"

During winter break of my senior year in college, I sat in a cold (OK, freezing!) tollbooth in the middle of the night wondering what the future held for me. Working the midnight shift as a toll collector (before the days of the E-ZPass) gave me an opportunity to meet some interesting characters heading toward downtown Boston. It also gave me plenty of time to think about life after college and what it might look like.

One morning, when I probably should have been resting after a long night's work, my mom and I took a train downtown to spend some time together. We stopped at a bookstore and I checked out the self-help aisle, figuring I *needed* some help determining the next steps in my life.

It was then that I came across the book *Live Your Dreams* by Les Brown, a world-renowned motivational speaker. The book instantly jumped out at me thanks to the red letters on its spine, and I knew I had to have it. My mom graciously paid for it, and I was off on a journey that has taken me places! In fact, I'm still on that journey of self-discovery and growth that started in 1997.

Many of Les's insights had an immediate impact on me and shaped how I would chart my life's course from that point on. After reading *Live Your Dreams*, I was determined to join the ranks of "unstoppable" people, as Les refers to them. I learned the power of affirmations and phrases that set the tone for both our conversations with ourselves and our interactions with others. I discovered the power of setting goals and pursuing them with passion.

Three months after reading *Live Your Dreams*, I had the incredibly good fortune of meeting Les Brown in person during a two-hour seminar in Washington, DC, where he was discussing the concepts in his book *It's Not Over Until You Win!* Listening to him speak was enthralling; I held onto his every word. I had a *"that's what I want to do when I grow up"* moment!

Four months after graduating from college, I came up with an idea in the middle of the night for a potential book to write. I wrote the word "SUCCESS" in capital letters on an index card, then wrote down one word for each letter in SUCCESS so that it would become a roadmap for goal setting and achievement:

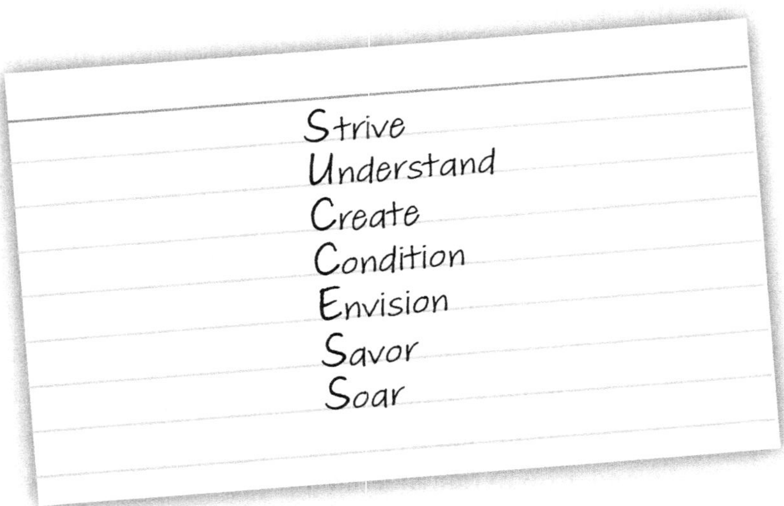

I put the index card away and let my ideas marinate over the next several months. Then, the following year, I began writing the manuscript for my new book-in-progress.

I was doing well for about fifty pages. But then I started coming down with "Who Am I?" Syndrome, thinking to myself: *"Who am I to write and publish a book at such a young age? Who am I to inspire others to live their dreams when I'm still working on my own?"*

At one point, I thought about letting the dream go; the journey was long and hard, and there were no guarantees that the SUCCESS book would *be* a success. But my wife (then girlfriend), Trevia, wouldn't let me give up so fast. I'll never forget what she said to me:

You have a message that people need to read.
Don't hit the delete button. Don't give up on your dream!

The question then became: *"Who am I to NOT listen to my soulmate?"* And so I heeded the sage advice of my better half and continued on the journey. Despite having been turned down by twenty-six traditional publishers, I was determined to learn the ropes of marketing and publishing and to get my book into print.

A year and a half later, I attended a conference in Silver Spring, Maryland. The keynote speaker was none other than ... Les Brown, the man who had inspired me to go after my dreams, one of which was to write and publish a motivational book. When Les came to my table before his presentation, I introduced myself and asked if he would consider writing the foreword to my upcoming book, *Spell SUCCESS in Your Life*, which was inspired by his book *Live Your Dreams*. "I'd be glad to!" he said, and he gave me his business card.

A few months later, I called Les to make sure he remembered agreeing to endorse my book, and he gave me his mailing address to send him a copy of the manuscript. A month went by with no word back from him; then another month. After the third month passed, I figured he was either too busy to get back to me or he had changed his mind.

In the meantime, I flew to Chicago for a week to attend Publishers Marketing University and Book Expo America, where I made some great connections in the publishing industry. I returned home exhilarated but exhausted.

And then it happened.

The next morning, the phone rang while I was still asleep. The name that showed up on the caller ID was ... "Brown, Leslie C."

Trevia picked up the phone.

"This is Les Brown," the voice on the other end said. "Could I speak to Peter, please?"

Trevia handed me the phone and said: "Les Brown is on the phone for you."

Thinking I was dreaming, I shook myself awake and said hello. And in his strong, bellowing voice, Les said: "Peter, this is Les. I've had a chance to read your book, and I love it! You can put my name all over it. I wish you much success on this project!"

I was speechless. But I managed to say thank you two or three times before we hung up. Getting Les Brown's endorsement felt like winning a jackpot!

Less than a year later, the first two thousand copies of my newly self-published book rolled off the press. And over the next few years, it was picked up by publishers in Argentina, Romania, China, India, Thailand, Indonesia, and South Korea. I even received a special e-mail from a grateful reader in India who wrote: "The pain you have taken to write this book has truly made a difference in my family's life." That one comment alone made it worth all the sweat and tears and late nights and rewrites.

The journey of my first book going from concept to completion had many twists and turns, but my dream eventually did flourish. How? Through the actions I took—sometimes on my own, often with the encouragement of others (Les Brown and Trevia being just two of the many)—that gave the dream space to breathe and drove it to grow.

▰ DREAMS EVENTUALLY FLOURISH ▰
by Peter Colwell

If you want your dreams to finally awaken
You must move ahead with belief unshaken
Resolving not to be mistaken
Thinking your destiny's forsaken.

Instead, march ahead to the beat of your drum
Faithfully following the sweet little hum
Of a yearning that is burning inside your soul
A feat you must complete to make you whole!

The future belongs to the dreamers who do.
To those who maintain a positive view
"Relentless" and "dogged" are traits of the few
Whose vision of greatness is bound to come true!

Many of your dreams will come to fruition
When you boldly follow your intuition
Overcoming any opposition
To align yourself with your life's true mission!

An April Fool's Exit to a Better Life

At times, we will find ourselves in a no-win situation, one that requires us to make a decision—and then take action—that will lead to sudden and important changes in our lives.

I once worked in a job that paid the bills but brought me no fulfillment or satisfaction. I stuck it out for as long as I could. But eventually, the stress of staying in an ill-fitting position manifested itself as chest pains. The doctor ruled out any health issues and chalked it up to stress. So I immediately knew what I had to do.

After consulting with Trevia (who was on board), I quit my job—on April Fool's Day, which happened to be no joke. Leaving the building that last time was a breath of fresh air and a new lease on life for me. The future was uncertain, but one thing was clear: I had control over my next steps, and I could be more selective about future job opportunities.

Four days later, the phone rang on a Friday morning. A temp assignment was available: answering phones for half a day. At first I resisted, thinking to myself: *"Why go in for half a day on a Friday when I can hit the ground running next week and look for a 'real job'?"* But Trevia reminded me that my last paycheck would run out soon, and so I switched gears and headed in for my half-day assignment, which involved working at a real estate company.

It turned out that I fit in well with the staff in the department, and they asked if I might be available for a few weeks to help out as needed around the office. Sure, I said.

At the end of the three weeks, no one approached me about my last day. I just continued helping people on projects, taking on more and more work with pleasure.

Three *months* later, I was informed that the department had maxed out its budget for temporary workers, but that another nearby office could really use some help.

Five months after that, everyone greeted me at the holiday party as the long-term temp.

Eventually, a full-time position opened at the original office where I had started—and that is where (and when) my real estate/property management career took off.

Five years into the field and one promotion later, my boss's boss advised me to "decide what you want. If this is the field where you really want to stay and grow, find people who are super successful and do what they're doing."

That's exactly what I did. A year later, my manager called and asked me to meet her outside the office. I hopped in her car, and we drove off to a nearby parking lot. Suddenly, she blurted out: "Do you want my job?" She was planning to move on as the result of a big promotion, and she needed to backfill her role. I accepted, and soon received a significant promotion to general manager, overseeing nine hundred thousand square feet of commercial office, industrial, and retail properties.

A Marked Turnaround

While things went very well initially, there were some growing pains in my new role—with one new client in particular.

As a new manager not yet seasoned in the art of proactive communication, I was struggling in silence with several issues instead of reaching out for help, which resulted in delays on some deliverables to the client. The client was thus dissatisfied with my service—something I hadn't experienced before.

I finally reached out to my manager, who had complete confidence in me. "You can turn this ship around," she said. "Show them that you *know* what you know. Perception is everything. Be proactive in your communication and be visible. Stay in front of every issue and keep them informed."

I followed her advice, making tiny tweaks in my communication style and reaching out proactively, and when I did the relationship improved dramatically. A month later, in fact, the client noted a marked turnaround, and they were thrilled with my performance.

Perhaps you, too, are going through a struggle, and your ship seems to be headed toward the proverbial iceberg. With a committed approach to excellence, built on action, you, too, can—and will—"turn the ship around"!

A Push Out of the Comfort Zone

A few years into my role as general manager, I had a good handle on the finances, operations, and overall management of the properties in my portfolio. Unfortunately, the financial downturn of 2008 and 2009 affected many commercial properties. In my case, more than half of the assets in my portfolio reverted to the lender. Amidst all the uncertainty, I started to wonder whether I'd still have a job.

Realizing I couldn't control external conditions and influences, I decided to put my worries aside and enjoy our upcoming family vacation in southern Maine—a respite that has brought me delight ever since I was a child, and has created beautiful memories for more than a decade of my adult life for me, my wife, my children, and my parents.

On the Monday morning after our vacation ended, I drove to work, envisioning what the day might look like. In my mind, I saw myself catching up with my coworkers, grabbing a cup of coffee, showing some pictures from our vacation, and then settling into work mode by checking all the e-mails I had purposely not read for the past ten days.

Instead, I received a phone call while I was on my way to the office. It was my boss. He asked me how my vacation went—then asked if it was safe for me to pull over to the side of the road.

I wasn't sure I liked where things were going, but I did as he asked.

He then gave me an address to plug into my GPS and advised me not to go into the office, but rather to drive directly to the address he'd specified—in the opposite direction, and in the next state over to boot.

I arrived at the location to find my boss and another executive. A few minutes later, they ... offered me a senior management position, which included oversight of the headquarters of the Department of Homeland Security as well as several other government agencies. It would be a significant increase in overall responsibility.

Instead of thinking things through and analyzing the pros and cons of the offer, I decided in that moment to go for it. They then welcomed me to my new position, which would start immediately, and said: "Congratulations! Now, go meet your staff."

For the next few years, I would oversee some significant projects for my new client and lead a team of hardworking engineers and administrative staff to recognition as Property Team of the Year.

And then, with changes in leadership, came an opportunity to be a regional operations manager, a role that truly aligned with my strengths: communication, employee training and development, and ensuring a smooth onboarding process for new employees.

Each progression in my career has been the result of saying yes to opportunities that aligned with my skills and talents.

My career moments of truth:

- Quitting my job with no backup, knowing it was worth it for my well-being.

- Deciding what I truly want and going for it with help from mentors.

- Saying yes to career leaps.

- Confronting concerns and enhancing communication.

- Saying yes to a huge opportunity—stretching my comfort zone.

- Saying yes again to a leap of faith to do work that better aligned with my skills.

That's how things have played out for me. The same (or even better) can happen for you, especially if you take action to remove yourself from toxic environments, identify what you really want, and open yourself up to new and exciting opportunities for growth.

Reflect on a moment of truth you've experienced in your career. How did you rise to the challenge, and what qualities did the experience bring out in you?

____

____

____

____

A Personal Leap of Faith

Trevia and I had been dreaming of owning a home since we'd gotten married in 2000. But various circumstances over the years—including our previous financial challenges and the housing bubble of the mid-2000s—had prevented us from realizing that vision.

Still, we were determined to keep this goal in the forefront of our minds. We always viewed it as a possibility, regardless of outward circumstances. We had a detailed list of the amenities our house would have, and we remained convinced that things would eventually turn around in our favor and that the right house would present itself at the right time.

In the fall of 2008, we made a one hundred percent commitment to moving into our ideal house by the spring of 2009. We'd given ourselves a firm deadline; now, all we had to do was come up with the funds and find the right house!

Market conditions began to work in our favor with a significant drop in housing prices and interest rates. Our funding fell into place with an unexpected and early bonus at work. After dozens of virtual tours and a handful of in-person visits, we stumbled upon the perfect house for us. We went to a nearby coffee shop right afterward to discuss it. We loved everything about it. Although we didn't have enough money for a big down payment, we decided to ignore the obstacles and "leap … and grow our wings on the way down."

Before our agent had made it all the way home, we called her and told her we wanted to make an offer on the house. She met us in her office that same evening and we filled out the initial paperwork.

Even though another offer had been made on the house, ours was accepted five days later. (Apparently, one of the co-sellers liked our handwriting and had a good feeling about us!)

The contract was a short sale, which, ironically, is not short in duration; in fact, short sales can take several months to settle. They can even fall through at any point, since the bank has little motivation to buy back a property at a discounted price.

But thanks to our agent (who was skilled in negotiating short sales) and some good luck, we were able to settle within three months.

The feeling as we left the settlement attorney's office and drove toward our new home for the first time was unmatchable—a slice of heaven!

In retrospect, there were several keys to our success:

- We knew what we wanted.

- We were convinced we would reach our goal.

- We stayed committed to our dream.

- We gave ourselves a firm deadline (positive pressure).

- We took a leap of faith.

What goal has been on your back burner for some time and perhaps needs to be revitalized? Maybe conditions have changed or improved so that you're closer to realizing it. Half of any achievement is first deciding what you want and being fully committed to it. *Commitment* and *passion* will fuel you to the finish line!

> *Until one is committed, there is hesitancy, the chance to draw back. Concerning all acts of initiative (and creation), there is one elementary truth, the ignorance of which kills count-less ideas and splendid plans: that the moment one defi-nitely commits oneself, then Providence moves too. All sorts of things occur to help one that would never have otherwise occurred. A whole stream of events issues from the decision, raising in one's favor all manner of unforeseen incidents and meetings and material assistance, which no man could have dreamed would have come his way. I learned a deep respect for one of Goethe's couplets: "Whatever you can do, or dream you can do, begin it. Boldness has genius, power, and magic in it." Begin it now!*
>
> W.H. MURRAY

Release Your Big Dream

If you step into a pair of shoes that is one or two sizes too small for you, most likely you will experience only a bit of discomfort and irritation. But when you set *goals* that are too small for you, just to play it safe and stay in your routine, you risk never knowing what you're truly capable of accomplishing.

The what-ifs, could'ves, and should'ves emerge from your sub-conscious mind. You begin to wonder: *"What if I'd tried out for the team?" "What if I had asked for a promotion?" "What if I'd stood up to that bully?"*

Small goals don't require much focus or energy. Neither do mediocre dreams. How can you "rise to the occasion" or "show people what you're made of" if you don't bother to put your skills and God-given abilities to the test?

The size of your dream and the measure of your success
will be in direct proportion to the depth of your belief.
PETER COLWELL

Think about your *big* dream: a dream that defines your deepest desire. Maybe even a dream you've been afraid to reveal to others, or that you've placed on the back burner—seemingly indefinitely. Write this dream down in detail, then describe why achieving it is important to you and how others would benefit from it.

When it comes to your dream, your big dream, you must put *all* your eggs in the basket of achieving it. Yes, you might be thinking: *"Wouldn't it be safer (and wiser) to have a couple of backup plans, in case my dream doesn't work out?"* It *is* good to have a backup plan for small goals and not-so-important dreams. But if you are truly committed to your one big dream, you must throw away the safety net—and leave yourself no other option *but* to succeed.

Rising to a Middle-of-the-Night Challenge

On the evening of February 10, 2010—a day I'll be telling my grandchildren about—a late-night phone call changed the course of my entire year.

As I was enjoying some rare quiet time with my wife, having a cup of coffee while our young children were asleep, the phone rang. It was my chief engineer, Jerry.

I knew right away that Jerry wasn't making a social call at 10 p.m. Instead, he told me that a large section of the roof of one of the warehouses I managed (a facility he oversaw from a mechanical perspective) had collapsed due to an extremely heavy snow load.

I instantly felt my heart sink. I gave Trevia a look that told her I'd be tied up for quite some time, and our "quiet" evening abruptly ended.

My mind started racing with thoughts of what I'd need to do next as I jotted down notes of what had occurred to that point. Offices were closed, of course, and my client would not likely hear about the incident until the morning. But I knew I needed to take some action before the sun rose.

I called my company's Crisis Connection Hotline and was fortunate to be put through to a gentleman named Frank who immediately put me at ease.

"Peter," he said, "I'm going to share a few action steps that you need to take just as soon as you can. Don't worry about anything else tonight except for these few items. Everything else can be addressed tomorrow and moving forward."

The first thing I needed to do was find, in the middle of the night, a structural engineer who could meet me on site first thing in the morning. Up until that point, I hadn't worked with a structural engineer, and thus I didn't have the name of anyone on file. So I called my assistant manager, and she jumped on the task and found a structural engineer who was willing and able to take on the challenge.

Next, I needed to contact emergency-response vendors and our snow removal contractor, since forty inches of snow had accumulated due to unprecedented back-to-back blizzards over a period of a few days.

Finally, I notified senior leaders within my company as well as our client, who would wake up to discover the news.

After an adrenaline-filled night, and functioning on only about ninety minutes of sleep, I headed out to the warehouse in treacherous road conditions the next morning. The highways had only one lane plowed, for emergency vehicle use only. I used that lane to travel to the property. It took twice as long as normal.

When I arrived, I met with the structural engineer and other contractors to assess the extent of the damage. Little did we know that when the roof had collapsed, it had broken two six-inch sprinkler lines, flooding the entire 265,000-square-foot warehouse. Water had been pouring out of the sprinkler lines at a furious clip for several hours throughout the night.

The scene in the warehouse was bleak, and we had our work cut out for us. The emergency-response vendors got things started, extracting water from the warehouse, isolating the utilities, and cleaning up as necessary. Fortunately, there were no fatalities in the incident, and much of the equipment in the warehouse was wrapped in plastic and resting atop pallets—otherwise the damage would have been much worse, and much more costly.

The next ninety-six hours involved continuous communication, emergency work, and round-the-clock strategizing to ensure the tenant would be able to resume operations the following week—with very few restrictions.

It was an event that required an all-hands-on-deck approach, and that's what our team provided at all levels. Our mettle was tested, and we rose to the challenge. The work would continue for the next twelve months, resulting in a $1.2 million reconstruction project that restored the space to full operation. Our team quickly got up to speed on insurance-claim matters and building-code standards. We were stretched to the limit and brought forth our very best efforts in communication and leadership, day in and day out.

A Brotherly Bond Is Born

Our emergency response to the roof collapse, along with our follow-up efforts, strengthened my leadership skills. But the experience also brought into my life a young man who would become one of my dearest friends.

On that snowy morning when I arrived at the warehouse, I shook hands with Mike Matthai, who, in his role as an emergency-response contractor, was waiting in front of the building. Mike's team quickly went to work extracting enormous amounts of water from the warehouse, speeding up the process of remediation—to the delight of my client.

While Mike and I became merely business contacts that day, fate would place us in a foursome on a golf course six years later. There, we would have an entire afternoon (and eighteen holes of golf) to get to know each other beyond just a name and a face. Mike and I don't remember playing any golf that day—we left most of that to the other two people in our group! But it was on the greens and fairways that we realized how similar our philosophies were. On that day, a friendship was truly born.

Mike and I formed a mastermind alliance to help each other in our personal and professional pursuits—and to minimize our respective risks and maximize our respective rewards as we pursued continued success. Our get-togethers since have been so meaningful and mesmerizing that we once had a restaurant waitress who had served us lunch ask us several hours later if we'd like to see the dinner menu!

Mike and I have shared many life-enhancing moments together, including attending events featuring Les Brown and Tony Robbins, inspiring senior citizens to live their best lives, and encouraging emerging leaders to build their self-esteem and push through their comfort zones.

A Deep Desire to Connect

Mike worked at a ski shop as a young man, and after reading *How to Win Friends & Influence People* by Dale Carnegie, he developed a deep desire to connect with others and create substantial relationships in his life. Sales representatives would come into his ski shop and get customers excited about the features and benefits of the products there. The reps also had the chance to travel and were respected as subject-matter experts. That was the kind of life and career Mike wanted to pursue.

He learned very quickly what selling truly entails, and that it's not just about the transaction and closing the deal; it's also about what happens after the sale ends—the follow-up. Sales is not a one-and-done undertaking. Rather, you build and sustain relationships, so that your customers very often become your friends.

Mike travelled coast to coast for five years teaching people about the selling process. Some of his best advice came from his own mentor:

- Do what you say you're going to do. Integrity is everything.
- Do the heavy lifting. It *will* pay off.
- Make other people's jobs easier.
- Remember that you don't know what you don't know. Keep learning.

Mike attributes his career longevity and stability to doing what he loves and what he *should* be doing. Some people do well in a certain role, but they're in the wrong industry. They are not truly the right fit; they are square pegs in round holes. When Mike, on the other hand, discovered a career in sales and then in business development, he navigated himself to *where he was meant to be*. He learned that 80 percent of success in life is showing up and putting yourself out there. The other 20 percent encompasses personality, attitude, and technical acumen, among other traits and skills. Industries can experience dramatic changes, practically overnight, from external conditions. So learning how to get things done is imperative when it comes to productivity and profitability in a career.

For some people, happiness equates to a big house on a hill and some beautiful cars. Others have a completely different vision and definition. When Mike was struggling in an unhealthy relationship early in his adult life, his mom said to him: "You're too young to be this unhappy." It's so important to get out of difficult situations and find a better fit. Take what you've learned and apply it intentionally toward your next step(s). Move forward with confidence—relying on inspired action to take you where you want to go!

Keep Showing Up

After eighteen years in commercial real estate, I tried my hand at residential real estate. While many of the skills I had developed over the years would continue to prove useful, I also needed to learn some new methods, techniques, protocols, and language to be successful in my role as a residential manager.

One of the keys to success when you're trying something new is to simply keep showing up each day, even when the strangeness of the new environment and its new expectations may tempt you to go back to the safe and the known, where the likelihood of success might be greater. But you need to do more than simply show up:

- You need to show up with a smile.
- You need to show up with commitment to your team.
- You need to show up with positive thoughts and encouraging words, for yourself and for others.
- You need to show up with humor, optimism, gratitude, compassion, and readiness for regular reflection.
- You need to show up after the shine of newness wears off and the "honeymoon period" is over.
- You need to show up when you're knee-deep in new challenges.

- You need to show up when things go against you.

- You need to show up when uncertainty abounds.

- You need to show up when you've made a mistake, and you need to be willing to own it.

- You need to show up and demonstrate your resilience.

Apply your knowledge intentionally to new situations. Trust your instincts. Your confidence and composure will begin to grow as you prove to yourself that you *can* create new successes in your life.

You don't have to get it right, you just have to get it going.

MIKE LITMAN

Have you ever heard the expression "give it a whirl"? It's an American colloquialism that dates to the late 1800s, and it refers to making an initial attempt without knowing how things will work out. To stretch in new directions, we must be willing to try—to take chances and engage in inspired action!

GIVE IT A WHIRL

by Peter Colwell

Are you tired and sick of it?
Stuck in the thick of it
Finally eager for change?

Daring to go for it
Willing to grow for it
Ready to broaden your range?

Your dreams can unfurl
If you'll "give it a whirl"
Your hopes can at last be fulfilled.

A great satisfaction
Is spurred from quick action
When negative voices are stilled.

The moment that makes you
Or suddenly breaks you
Is truly one of a kind. ...
Don't ever forget ... your destiny's set
The moment you make up your mind!

Like Minds Combine to Shine

Several years ago, during a management conference in Arizona, I sat in a tavern next to a colleague I barely knew. Her name was Carol Stauffer. She had a delightful smile and a positive spirit, and she was highly approachable.

Previously, I had known Carol only by her name, and only from a distance. But that night, she and I really got to know each other in a comfortable, relaxed environment—many miles away from the properties we managed on the East Coast of the United States.

A few months later, Carol and I participated in what would be an eight-month leadership course that focused on emotional intelligence, self-awareness, and leadership styles. The two of us became accountability partners. We participated in the exercises, followed up with each other routinely, and helped each other stay on task. We knew we had great rapport going when we would meet for lunch and laugh so hard it hurt. One time, we even needed to move to another section of the deli so that we wouldn't disrupt the other customers!

Aligned with the timing of this course was the emergence of a regional leadership development program, which Carol and I co-created along with a couple of other senior leaders in the organization. A year and a half into the program, we received national recognition for it with a nomination for a Real Estate Management Excellence award for innovation in employee and leadership development.

We showed up for the national awards dinner, thankful that our program had been well-received and grateful to be in the running with other notable leadership development initiatives. With several hundred people in the audience, organizers announced the nominees—and then our program ... as the winner! Carol was getting out her camera to take a picture of our program's name on the big screen. I nudged her: "Hey, we just won! We need to get onstage while they're still playing the music!" In disbelief and sudden joy, we walked briskly to the stage to accept our award.

It soon became apparent that Carol and I were destined to collaborate in multiple ways: to serve emerging leaders within our department, region, and organization; and to serve the industry as a whole via educational courses and seminars. The merging of our minds would lead to the creation of content that would offer audiences inspiration, take-back-to-work strategies, and new methods for dealing with common obstacles in the workplace.

While Carol and I are no longer colleagues, we continue to fill each other's tanks with words of hope and encouragement as each of us embarks on new adventures. We're rooting each other on from afar!

Grab the Next Fingerhold!

Carol is not afraid of challenges—and she *never quits*. When she falls down, she keeps getting back up.

Early in her career, she went from job to job until she fell into, and embraced, a career in property management. She was invited to take a position answering phones because someone loved her voice. She gravitated toward opportunities to talk to people and make circumstances better. Her people skills and her ability to handle situations with professionalism have served her well her entire career. Her honesty, dependability, and transparency—as well as her willingness to take on new responsibilities—have powered her career from administrative roles to the senior management ranks.

When adversity strikes, Carol's response is: "Bring it on!" As a newborn, Carol wasn't even expected to survive. But her parents prayed for her to get through her health challenges, and she did just that.

Her life since has reflected that inner strength and determination. In her younger years, she tried a lot of things out to see what she was truly passionate about, but her belief in God slowly clarified her thoughts while giving her the ability to stretch when she needs to.

Carol once went mountain climbing and rappelling with her three children. At the beginning of the climb, she looked at the mountain and had no idea how she'd make it to the top. Her children kept telling her: *"Grab the next fingerhold. Don't think about it. Don't look around. Just grab that next fingerhold."* And before long, Carol had scaled the mountain with her kids—one of the most satisfying moments of her life.

But then she had to figure out how to get back down.

She had to rappel—lean back and drop. But she relied on the resilient attitude that is engrained in her, the one that has produced results for her so many other times in her life.

Carol is at her best when things are going against her and seem to be falling apart. She leans on the phrase: "As a man thinketh in his heart, so is he." Our circumstances will eventually change. When we focus continually on the positive side of life, there is almost always a silver lining. Carol professes the positive, which eventually results in a changed behavior(s), which in turn leads to a more optimal outcome most of the time.

Carol once had to take a difficult exam for professional credentials. She failed it the first time. And the second. The third time, she said to herself: *"Something's gotta change!"* So she paid the exam fee (again) but changed the way she approached her preparation for the test. She studied more diligently, for starters. More importantly, though, she cut out a picture of herself with a huge smile on her face and placed index cards all over her house that said: *"I passed! I passed!"* She carried that mind picture as she was studying.

The result: The third time was a charm; she not only passed the test, she did so with a very high mark.

If you've stumbled or faced a setback recently, picture yourself succeeding. Surround yourself with competent, confident, action-oriented people like Carol. Their energy and enthusiasm will rub off on you!

> *If we all did the things we are really capable of doing, we*
> *would literally astound ourselves.*
> THOMAS EDISON

SEEDS OF FAITH
by Peter Colwell

Finding

An

Iota of

Trust and

Hope

Getting a grip ... on the end of your rope!
An uncertain future is about to unfold.
Remember that "fortune favors the bold."

What happens from here is up to your mind.
Will you dare to move forward ... or shrink and rewind?
Will your thoughts encourage you to a stronger belief?
Or will they betray you and exacerbate grief?

The seeds of a prosperous new beginning
Will only flourish with a mindset of winning
Victory is at hand for those who believe
That their inner genius is about to conceive.

With faith as your fuel and hope as your guide,
Adventure awaits! Enjoy the ride!

3

KEY TAKEAWAYS
from Chapter Two

1. The pressures of the moment are temporary.
    A "move!" mindset will keep you going
    during difficult times.

2. Applying knowledge intentionally helps
    us create new successes in our lives.

3. To grow your wings, take a leap of faith
    and embrace the outer edges of your
    comfort zone.

Whatever It Takes

by Peter Colwell

A very sound philosophy
To help us get good breaks
Can all at once be uttered by the words
"whatever it takes."

Quintessential to our growth
is greater understanding
Of what it takes to hit the mark
and nail a perfect landing.

A skill refined through daily grind
A will that will not cower
Creation of a mastermind
To find our superpower!

Through all life's trials and travails
Remember this one fact:
That hope persists and love prevails
In keeping us intact!

chapter three

Navigate Through Negativity

*Negative inner dialogue is like a computer virus that
infects the operating system, damaging or destroying it.
On a human level, it's the equivalent of distorting
the truth of your personal worth and value.*

ARNOLD SANOW

Have you ever fallen prey to your own thoughts and words—talking yourself out of doing something you really want to try, wondering if you really have what it takes, coming up with a litany of excuses for why you don't have the time, or rationalizing to yourself that "it probably won't work"?

I have.

On a Monday evening in September when my son, Petey, was six years old and just entering first grade, I brought him to our middle school for "Join Scouting Night" to enroll him in the Cub Scouts as a Tiger Scout. As a child, I'd had great experiences in Scouting, and my hope was that Petey might also have the opportunity to build his character, citizenship, and love of the outdoors through Scouting.

After offering an overview of the program, the Cubmaster asked the boys in attendance to go to another room to play, so that the adults could talk about, presumably, "adult stuff."

Once the kids were gone, the Cubmaster got right to the point.

"Look, our reason for meeting tonight is simple," he said. "We need volunteers to be Den Leaders so we can start up two Tiger Dens. I know you're all busy with work and family responsibilities, but we can't have a program without new volunteers."

As much as I wanted to get involved and be a part of my son's growth and development in Scouts, I rationalized—with a strong argument to justify it—that I was too busy. After all: I had just received a big promotion at work, and along with that promotion came lots of new responsibilities consuming my time and attention. I didn't want to set myself—or the boys I'd be leading—up for failure.

What if I started strong but ran out of steam? What if I couldn't keep up with delivering the requirements of the program? What if my ideas weren't creative enough? What if ... what if ... what if ...?

I decided not to raise my hand.

I told myself (quietly) that if the group needed help at a particular event, I could step in. But a continuous, weekly commitment of my time (and preparation and debriefing) seemed like too much to take on. I looked around, hoping a couple of the other attendees would jump in instead. But similar conversations must have been going on in the minds of the other parents, who were undoubtedly stretched with responsibilities and activities of their own.

Finally, the Cubmaster said: "Let me remind you that, without any volunteer leaders, we cannot have a program for your boys."

Suddenly, the thought of Petey missing out on fun, adventure, and learning was more distressful than the thought of taking on this new task. So, without flinching, my left arm started to levitate—halfway up ... then all the way.

"I'll do it," I said.

Then another few hands went up, and moments later we had ourselves two Tiger Dens with leaders.

That pivotal moment resulted in a five-year leadership journey for me; I was a Den Leader for four years and then served an additional year as the Cubmaster of a pack of one hundred boys. We organized visits to museums, police and fire stations, and a local TV studio. We went on hikes and family camping trips that we will long remember and cherish. Skits, games, and friendly competitions were all part of our regular meetings.

My wife, Trevia, stepped up to be my co-leader, and together we had a unique, wonderful chance to be part of Petey's life during his elementary school years, and to proudly watch him grow from boy to adolescent and, ultimately, to a fine young man who worked his way up the ranks to Eagle Scout.

If I had allowed my negative inner dialogue to talk me out of stepping up to lead, I would have missed out on so many life-enriching experiences with my son, not to mention all the other boys I had a chance to influence during those amazing years.

Self-doubt is one of the primary reasons people don't follow through on what they've started (or even start at all). At some point in the midst of working toward a goal, they lose confidence in themselves and abandon their efforts altogether.

This is what happens when we question ourselves and our abilities. If you could turn off the "doubt switch" inside your head, you'd have more abundance, be more creative, and feel more fulfilled. You'd also have the satisfaction of finishing what you start, and consequently you would feel better about yourself.

Wouldn't it be great if we really could simply turn off a switch and eliminate our feelings of worthlessness and self-doubt? While there is no such physical switch, of course, we do have the capacity to turn off the doubt switch in our minds.

For many of us, the process needs to begin by reassessing—and perhaps changing—who we spend our time with and how we let ourselves be influenced by them.

Doubt destroys. Belief builds.
PETER COLWELL

Negative Types Are Everywhere—BEWARE!

Virtually all of us come across people who try, knowingly or perhaps unwittingly, to counteract our positive spirit. The moment they realize we are happy-go-lucky and have a can-do attitude, they try to bring us down to their emotional level.

If we fail to guard ourselves against the negative words and actions of negative people, we risk paying a steep price in terms of our emotional health and well-being, not to mention our psychological safety. Just as we would protect our house from a potential invader, our children from avoidable accidents, and our belongings from possible theft, we should steer clear of—or at least delicately handle—the various forms of negative behavior we regularly encounter. With foresight and awareness, we can successfully navigate through negativity.

Let's look at several examples of the negative personalities and behaviors you'll want to avoid (or at least learn to manage) to minimize pain and disruption in your life and instead keep yourself happy and healthy—physically, mentally, emotionally, and spiritually.

Beware of the Caution Police

Most of the time, members of the Caution Police are well-meaning. But their overly tentative approach can limit your potential for personal development.

The Caution Police can appear in the form of a parent, sibling, or friend advising you against making a move because they deem it too risky. They may come up with a string of potential reasons why your plan won't work and then urge you to play it safe.

But there are times in life when you need to take a calculated risk—to advance in your career, for instance, or to grow as a person. It's up to you to weigh the pros and cons of making an important decision, and to rely on your instincts, knowledge, and inner guidance to reveal the right path to you.

When you're faced with a critical choice, one that could lead you in several possible directions, be sure to mentally and physically step away from the situation—and the Caution Police!—so that you can explore your needs and wants. Here are a few questions that will help you:

- What do I truly want (or think I truly want)?
- Why do I want this?
- Will having or achieving this truly make me happy?
- If so, why? If not, why not?

It may help to write these questions down and then let the answers come to you. You'll often find that insights pop up at unusual times and in unexpected places. A conversation with someone or a routine, everyday task may trigger the answers you're looking for.

Your answers.

When I graduated from college, I was offered what I considered to be a golden opportunity: a summer internship with the Criminal Division of the Office of International Affairs, part of the U.S. Department of Justice (DOJ) in Washington, DC. While it was an unpaid position, I viewed it as a short-term way to gain credible work experience, build my professional network, and see where things might go from there.

When I shared the news of the internship with the people close to me, most of them were happy for me and supportive of the new endeavor. But someone within my inner circle at the time suggested I should forego the opportunity to instead find something more definitive, long-term, and income-producing.

At that point in my life, I was more concerned with accumulating work experience and getting to know people. And the opportunity itself seemed like an excellent resume-builder. So I accepted it and jumped into my new role with enthusiasm.

I made some great connections at DOJ, for starters. I also made such a positive impression on the leadership there that they asked me to stay an extra month to help with their heavy workload.

To help pay the bills during the internship, I worked evenings and weekends as a bellman at a local hotel.

The connections I made and the ideas I generated that summer led me to additional career-enhancing opportunities—and to the writing of my first book, *Spell SUCCESS in Your Life: A Road Map for Achieving Your Goals and Surviving Success* (Dreams Unlimited Press, 2002).

Don't let even well-meaning people talk you out of taking chances if you feel you're making the right move. As the ancient Roman poet Virgil once said: "Fortune favors the bold."

Who are some members of your Caution Police squad? How can you deal with their overwhelming concern and make sure you don't allow them to talk you out of an opportunity that feels right for you?

____

____

____

Beware of the How Detective

Have you ever dealt with someone who, the moment you reveal your plans and goals, comes up with a long list of questions beginning with the word "how"?

As in:

- "How are you going to live on your own when you can't even cook a meal for yourself?"

- "How are you going to become an entrepreneur when you have no business experience?"
- "How are you going to be a talk show host someday when you're afraid to speak in public?"

Shortly after airing their list of hows, these folks generally tell you why you can't, shouldn't, and/or won't make it happen for yourself. They're almost desperate to convince you to back away from your plans because—in their minds, at least—there are too many questions and too few answers.

How Detectives are curious and inquisitive about your motives. How on earth, they wonder, will you possibly achieve your goals? They expect a detailed, step-by-step plan before they can give you their seal of approval and support.

In reality, the only question you need to ask yourself about your aspirations is "why?" Once you know your why and you have it firmly planted in your subconscious mind, you can go about the business of making your dreams come alive through persistent, daily actions toward the outcome you want.

Let the How Detectives "how?" someone else! Focus instead on your why—and on fulfilling the purpose and aspirations that spring from it!

Starting with WHY is what inspires people to act.
SIMON SINEK

What is a purpose you must fulfill, a feat you must complete? And WHY?

____

____

____

Beware of the Ego Deflater

If you've ever come across an Ego Deflater, you know that this pessimistic personality seems to have a dual mission in life:

1. To make you feel as worthless as possible.

2. To make himself/herself feel superior to you in the process.

Without delving into the reasons behind this type of behavior (we want to keep this book to a reasonable length!), let's focus on how to counteract it. Here are four proven ways for dealing with the downers in your life:

Remember the sage advice of Eleanor Roosevelt: "No one can make you feel inferior without your consent." Repeat these words to yourself when you're forced to confront an Ego Deflater. These people love to rain on your parade and spoil a good moment.

Let's say you've just completed an educational course that is not related to your field of study and not likely to directly lead to employment in a traditional job. You may hear comments like *"Why did you waste your time taking that course? It's not going to get you anywhere!"* Or *"I could think of better ways to spend my time."* Don't let such feedback deter you from doing what makes you happy.

Separate other people's opinions from your self-image. Don't take the Ego Deflater's comments personally. Realize that other people's opinions of you do not have to dictate your reality.

Surround yourself with ego boosters—people who regularly remind you about your positive qualities and achievements. I even keep a "kudos" box at home with notes and letters from my own ego boosters: friends, family, and colleagues who have congratulated me on accomplishments or just wished me well. These notes pick me up when I'm having a bad day.

Become your own ego booster. Don't rely solely on others to make you feel good about yourself. Treat yourself the way you'd treat a good friend or a family member you love: Say the same nice things to (and about!) yourself that you would say to (and about!) them.

What can you do to give yourself a much-needed boost? Who else in your life can you call on to cheer you forward?

____

____

____

Beware of the Emotional Scrooge

You undoubtedly remember the famous movie *A Christmas Carol*, based on the novel by Charles Dickens. One of the major characters in the movie (and the novel) is Ebenezer Scrooge, a man known for his remarkable stinginess when it comes to giving money to other people.

The Emotional Scrooge withholds not money but love, compassion, kind words, encouragement, and praise. Instead of telling you how great you're doing, the Emotional Scrooge says nothing or leaves you wondering about—and perhaps doubting—yourself and your abilities.

Do you have an Emotional Scrooge in your life? If so, here are some ways to counteract the negative effects:

- Focus on spending time with people who will and do give you emotional support and encouragement.

- Try providing emotional support to the very person denying it to you. Who knows? Maybe you'll see a miracle unfold by applying the Golden Rule: *"Do unto others as you would have them do unto you."*

- Associate yourself with people who are physically and emotionally affectionate.

Often, we toil away in hopes of receiving recognition from others (private or public). We want to be noticed for our efforts. This is perfectly natural and understandable. In fact, many people prefer recognition over money and material possessions. (Personally, I would like all of the above!)

You'd be surprised how far people will go to receive recognition. All too often, we even hear of people who "go off the deep end" or become notorious in society. Frequently, these people simply want to be noticed. Their need for attention generally stems, at least in part, from a childhood absent of the essentials: love, compassion, kindness, support, understanding.

What can we learn from the Emotional Scrooges in our lives— and their opposites? If you're a parent, tell your children you love them. Don't let a day go by without saying to them—and, most importantly, showing them—that you love them, and that they are special to you. Learn from your children, too, as they so often demonstrate how natural and easy it is to show affection.

Who in your inner circle can give you a "warm and fuzzy" feeling? Who admires you for you? Schedule your next gathering with this person(s) now!

Beware of the Snark Shark

The Snark Shark is a toxic personality—one that's out for blood (though not literally, of course).

Snark Sharks pick up on any uncertainty or insecurity you're showing and prey upon it to their advantage. They make cutting remarks, hoping to get a reaction from you. They want you to lose your cool. They love keeping you off balance.

Snark Sharks use verbal aggression to make you feel helpless or inferior. They enjoy putting you on the spot and shaming you. They may bite you unexpectedly with cynical sarcasm or cheap verbal shots to diminish your efforts.

Watch out when Snark Sharks smile; they are merely showing you their teeth. A jab is likely to follow. They want their words to sting and to leave a mark.

But only you can determine if that mark will remain. You must rise up boldly and confidently against such menacing behavior and kill Snark Sharks with kindness. Give them what they need (which is loving-kindness), not what they want (a chance to rile you up and to feel falsely and temporarily superior to you).

When the situation becomes unbearable, get out of the environment where the Snark Shark is lurking. Towel up. Go to a safe place, just as you would if you were in danger of encountering a real shark in the ocean. Surround yourself with a shark cage of positive influence and support from people who know you, get you, and respect you. Build up your self-belief once again if your confidence has been shaken. Remain true to your innermost values, and don't allow the Snark Shark's behavior to change your essence.

Empower yourself with words and images that help you believe for a better day. Remember who you are and whose you are. You are greater than anything life throws at you—and that includes the Snark Shark!

Silence is golden. Brevity is best. What are some quick, noncombative replies you can have ready for the next Snark Shark attack you face?

____

____

____

Beware of the Chronically Cantankerous

If you've ever worked in customer service or dealt with a wide variety of people in other personal and/or professional settings, you've undoubtedly come across those who are among the ranks of the Chronically Cantankerous. These folks are itching for a fight; they arrive before you ready to blow up in your face, and they have an edginess to them that is unsettling and off-putting.

Despite other people's attempts to show them a little kindness, the Chronically Cantankerous focus on what agitates them and get angry rather quickly. If you find yourself in the wrong place at the wrong time with them (at their high point of irritability), you may become the target of verbal threats, which may or may not relate to something you've actually done. Oftentimes, the Chronically Cantankerous will unleash a tirade of complaints in your direction, leaving you little choice but to endure them until the show is over.

De-escalating the situation when you're faced with crotchety behavior can be a challenge. Keeping your cool and neutralizing your emotions (as much as possible) is perhaps the most effective way you can counteract someone's short fuse. A level head will help you quickly assess the situation and determine your (and others') level of safety and whether the conversation should continue or be cut short. You can then take a few moments to think about what you're going to say and how.

Many years ago when I was an assistant property manager, I had to confront a tenant who was known for his uncooperative spirit. My manager was out of the country, so I was asked to oversee a construction project during her absence and to handle any sensitive issues that might come up.

Everything was quiet for most of my manager's absence, until ... the unruly tenant got riled up. Some construction we were doing—construction we had preplanned and coordinated with him in advance—got underway one day. But the tenant changed his mind about it once the workers began, saying he didn't want the project to be completed (even though it needed to be done so that another tenant could move in legally).

The man raised his voice very loudly and shouted obscenities at the crew members, who were only there to do their jobs. So with my heart beating rapidly, I approached him and said firmly: "You will NOT speak to these people this way! You will treat everyone in this room with respect. This is NOT the Jerry Springer Show!"

The tenant immediately backed down and walked away. He came back a few minutes later much calmer, and the work continued as planned.

While I certainly would have preferred to avoid this Chronically Cantankerous man altogether, a face-to-face confrontation was necessary to resolve the matter. I grew some "leadership wings" that day—and I had a great "you're not going to believe this" story to tell my manager when she returned!

When you're faced with an unavoidable encounter with someone who tends to be cantankerous more often than not, collect yourself and show up with confidence that you will do and say the right thing, guided by your conscience and with the support of others who have your back.

How can you practice remaining neutral when others try to provoke an argument?

____

____

____

Replace Your Limiting Beliefs with Self-Affirming Ones

Spend enough time with people who worry, stew, gripe, withhold, diminish, yell—people who magnify problems and minimize possibilities—and you yourself will eventually fall into negative holding patterns. You'll wrestle with limiting beliefs, which invariably lead to self-doubt, anxiety, fear, insecurity, and despair.

Here are just a few examples of the ones you might be dealing with now, quite possibly without being aware of it:

- "There's only so much money out there."

- "Don't expect too much out of life. You might be disappointed."

- "You're not smart enough to hold that position."

- "Nobody in your family has ever done that before."

- "You're never going to make something of yourself."

To achieve the outcomes you want in life, sooner or later you'll need to challenge your limiting beliefs, whether you've developed them on your own or unknowingly adopted them from others.

If you are inundated by limiting thoughts and feelings each day, you need to actively and consciously decide to replace them with positive, self-affirming ones—attributes like confidence, love, courage, hope, and conviction.

It likely won't be easy, so ask for help: The listening ear of a friend or a professional counselor (or both) when things get overwhelming can provide the objectivity and perspective you need to start feeling (and thinking) better.

"I BELIEVE!"

by Peter Colwell

Two simple words when side by side
Expressed with confidence and pride
Will reinforce what you'll achieve
These simple words are ... "I believe!"

Acceptance that a thing is true
Backed by a willingness to do
Will steer you over, 'round and through
Past ANYTHING life throws at you.

That may include the "kitchen sink"
Uneasiness that makes you think
You have to run away and shrink
But wait, there is a missing link!

Determination to succeed
Readiness to finally lead
A life that reaches your potential
With passion that is exponential!

Tap into your inner sage.
Write your story—page by page.
Tell your fears at once to cease.
Make your life a masterpiece!

Getting to a Happy, Healthy Place

When life throws us off track, and we find ourselves moving in the opposite direction of the course we've envisioned for ourselves, our emotional and physical well-being can suffer. How lucky we are, then, when we encounter someone who can lift us back up— someone who gives us the tools and resources we need to once again steer our minds and bodies in a better direction.

Several winters ago, I had the great fortune of meeting such a person: Dr. Diane Kern. Diane was a guest corporate presenter who talked about how to counteract the stress that comes with deadlines to meet before year-end, as well as how to handle the positive and negative stress of planning for holiday events and gatherings. Diane also covered the loneliness and isolation experienced during the holidays by people separated from loved ones or grieving a loss.

Diane's words and mannerisms resonated with me intellectually and emotionally. A budding friendship gained a foothold that day, and we have met frequently ever since to spur each other on to greater heights in our careers and deeper richness in our personal lives.

Diane is a licensed therapist, facilitator, and author who helps people lift themselves up and create and sustain emotional well-being. A desire to help people led Diane to the field of psychology. It's a calling that has been deeply influenced by a strong family legacy of helping others. At an early age, Diane was taught: *"With whatever God has blessed you, you should share some, save some, and spend some."* Her mom believed in having balance, and part of that balance is sharing your blessings with others.

Diane's mother, Roxie Mills Kern, grew up in a farm family. Roxie was a black woman in the Jim Crow South who eventually became a teacher. She was grateful for the job because her opportunities were extremely limited. Even though she had a college degree, jobs were scarce because the South was segregated and the North was "de facto" segregated.

When Roxie migrated from Alabama to Ohio, she tried to get another job. The positions for black teachers had already been filled, so she had a difficult time. Eventually Roxie ended up working in a cafeteria, meeting Diane's father, and getting married.

Roxie was a stay-at-home mother for the first eleven years of Diane's life. When her marriage fell apart, she took her children to Syracuse, New York, to be near family. This was during the Lyndon B. Johnson era, when opportunities were opening up for African Americans and efforts were being made to recruit talented, qualified black people. These were significant cultural differences compared to the days when Diane was younger.

Roxie got yet another teaching job. She assumed her daughter would do the same, since that's the world she knew. Teaching was a respectable profession that could ensure career security. And security was important to Roxie: She knew firsthand the limitations of the society she grew up in; the career options for African American women were limited to nurse or teacher.

But thanks to the social changes of the 1960s, opportunities had opened up considerably—including in the field of psychology, which had not typically been welcoming or available to those of modest means.

When Diane was exposed to psychology, she began to understand the nature of human behavior and motivation, which piqued her curiosity. She would not have been satisfied or happy working in a classroom environment, she says. And she couldn't get rid of the thought that there were people out there who needed something far beyond general attention.

That's what ultimately compelled Diane to pivot to psychology (with related interests in sociology and journalism). She majored in psychology as an undergraduate and then got into a graduate clinical psychology program. Her primary aim: to become a therapist.

Diane was (and still is!) deeply interested in how people function, work, and think, and that led her to experiment with a variety of nontraditional endeavors. Eventually, though, she realized she was most curious about the notion of people being happy with their work.

Her first professional consultation job was with Goodwill Industries, an organization that prepares people with disabilities for the workforce. Diane quickly became the resident psychologist to handle crises. Her primary role was to augment the organization's training programs. She saw that therapy clients were unhappy with, and distressed about, their jobs because they weren't doing things that brought them joy. Diane felt fortunate to do something that fit her passion, and she began to see that other people could do the same thing—an enjoyable mission for her!

The psychology field, which has traditionally focused on distress and pathology, slowly began to embrace the Eastern philosophies, and meditation became part of the field's common discourse. The term "spirituality" wasn't even allowed in Diane's practice in the 1970s and '80s because of concerns it might be perceived as proselytizing and judgmental toward clients. But today, spirituality is at the core of Diane's work.

Rewrite Your Inner Dialogue

Diane's clients often need to work on changing their inner dialogue from negative to positive. You might be in the same boat, trying to figure out how to navigate through some sort of negativity in your life.

Diane's advice: Become your own best friend.

How would you talk to your best friend (or a protégé, or your own child)? You'd be kind, understanding, empathetic, patient. But we tend to treat *ourselves* according to a double standard: Most of us show far more grace and compassion toward others than we do to ourselves. Not only is that unfair; it's unhealthy and unsustainable.

Our tendency toward negative inner dialogue also affects us in terms of our self-control. It's difficult (indeed impossible sometimes!) to focus on what you *want* to do when the chatterbox in your head is constantly yammering about what you *don't* want to do or what you *shouldn't* do!

So if you want to gain more self-control, Diane says—monitor your diet, get more exercise, think more clearly—you need to get still within your spirit. Quiet the noise around you and refocus on yourself. Engage in meditation and clear the clutter swirling in your mind. Relax—in the real sense, where you redirect your energy toward something that will calm you, engage you, and allow you to center yourself. For example:

- Take a walk.

- Sit still in nature.

- Light a campfire.

- Spend fifteen minutes a day restoring yourself and recharging your batteries.

- Acknowledge that you are the engine of your own car: Neglect it and it will start making noises; you'll be lucky to trip a warning light before it's too late.

Starve Negative People of Their Power

Diane speaks, facilitates, and writes. She knows the power of words: They can edify us—or they can tear us down.

How do you deal with destructive words, particularly when they are hurled at you by someone else? Diane has some advice: **Don't give power to someone else's negative agenda.** Don't join forces with your adversary and jump on their wagon against you. Sometimes, in fact, the words people say to you and the actions they take toward you have nothing to do with you.

So when they come, challenge them. Ask yourself: *"Where is the evidence? On what basis is this person making this claim/accusation/ etc.?"* Take the other person out of the equation, Diane advises, and go to the substance of his/her statement. If there is no evidence to back the statement up, you will realize emotionally that it isn't true. And that assessment will help you get to the other side of being stuck on it.

Then you can ask yourself: *"What IS true? What can I point to and know about myself, based on experience, that will give me a more realistic idea of whether my dreams can come true, and how?"*

Don't be distracted by criticism. Remember: The only taste of success some people have is when they take a bite out of you.
ZIG ZIGLAR

HOPE

by Peter Colwell

Holding
On through
Prayer and
Expectation

Living with joy and animation ... That's hope!

Expressing our vitality
Exuding positivity
That's hope!

Hope has a friend called faith in action
Set into motion to give us traction.

Hope is a chance to be inspired
To let our negative thoughts get rewired.

Hope is not hype.
It's here to stay
Helping us to navigate each day.

So never give up, and never give in ...
Because it's not over ... until you win!

Valleys and Peaks, Peaks and Valleys

One day, you can be on top of the world. The next, the world can crumble beneath your feet.

One Thursday afternoon, I was delivering a keynote speech to nearly one hundred real estate association professionals. The topic: how to thrive during uncertain times, and how to stay motivated regardless of your circumstances. I reveled in the laughter and applause of the audience and in the warm connections I made afterward.

The very next day, my family and I would begin a protracted mental, emotional, and physical test that would drag on for a grueling ten weeks.

My dad, who had recently undergone a medical procedure, began the morning suffering the ill effects of an implantation gone wrong. That evening, he collapsed to the ground and was unable to put a coherent sentence together.

Fearing he'd had a stroke, my mom called an ambulance, and Dad was rushed to the hospital in downtown Boston. All our immediate family (including my son and me) flew into town to be with him.

After his condition stabilized over the next few days—and a stroke had, thankfully, been ruled out—my dad was transferred to a rehab facility. There, unfortunately, his health declined rapidly over the next five days, to the point he was unable to bring a spoon up to his mouth to eat.

The extreme lack of attention and concern he received at that facility almost proved to be fatal. We demanded further blood tests, knowing something wasn't right. Doctors at the facility finally relented and, based on the test results, my dad was rushed right back to the hospital where he'd been days earlier.

This time around, the medical team pressed for more answers to the confounding and complex health problems my dad was experiencing. After another period of stabilization—and without having all the answers—they released Dad to a different rehabilitation facility (it was a no-brainer he wouldn't be returning to the first one).

After just a day and a half at the second rehab facility, it was very clear to me that my dad's condition was deteriorating quickly. He was cowering in a wheelchair, unable to respond to us, and he was in intense pain. While I had no idea what was going on with him—nor did the staff at the facility—I knew instinctively that he would not survive long unless quick action was taken to return him *yet again* (for the third time in two weeks) to the hospital.

The staff at the rehab facility seemed convinced my dad was OK. But I knew that what I was seeing was not his baseline of health and physical abilities.

So, feeling like a bit of a madman in doing so, I motioned to the front-desk staff that they needed to call an ambulance quickly so that my dad could be driven to the hospital to receive emergency medical treatment.

When the emergency responders arrived, they asked me what was wrong. I admitted that I didn't have a definitive answer. I just knew my dad was declining.

We followed Dad back to the hospital, where he underwent numerous tests. They revealed a serious infection, one that would require immediate surgery to save his life.

Within hours, my dad had the surgery—and he was finally on the road, albeit an arduous one, to recovery. Ahead of him was six weeks of rehab at a third—and much better—facility that would help him regain his strength and mobility to walk again, and improve his mental clarity and cohesion. Dad did great there, and today he is mentally alert and walking around town every day— back to his normal ways!

The extreme medical challenge my dad endured required a dedicated team of medical professionals and an army of earthly angels to come to Dad's aid—and to relieve our stress as family members as we took care of him and developed a road map to improve his health. My dad's experience was full of sudden twists and scary turns, and it ultimately resolved itself through the power of prayer, the devotion of loved ones, and the steady hand of his medical team.

When we face sudden setbacks or crises that deplete our energy, incapacitate us for a while, and diminish our quality of life, it's hard to think positively and envision better days ahead. But even in these difficult and stressful circumstances, we can find a way to create space that allows us to imagine a better future and predict an upswing in our lives.

The way we navigate through the negativity can be as simple as saying to ourselves: *"WHEN I get home, I'll watch my favorite show and indulge with a bowl of ice cream."* Or: *"WHEN I get home, I'll get out the lawnmower and cut the grass, then lounge in my Adirondack chair in the backyard with a glass of lemonade."* The key word in these affirmative statements is "when." There are no "ifs," "buts," or "maybes."

You can also manage the downturns of life by focusing on what *is* working, what *is* going well. There may be nine things going wrong and only one thing going right. Where is your focus? How about dwelling on the one thing that brought you joy, or surprised you, or made you comfortable?

Taking stock of what's working serves us well in good times and lean times—during the ups *and* the downs of life. We may be in the valley for a long while before ascending to the peak. We can use that time wisely to develop patience and an appreciation of the simple things that nourish us and sustain our souls.

We are constantly navigating new challenges in life. With a positive, determined mindset, we can and will find our way to the other side of the adversity we face.

Make it a point to cast aside whatever might be weighing you down in a given moment, and take time to empty out your negative thoughts. Work toward a feeling of lightness, even during the dark times, so that you can rejuvenate and restore yourself, readying yourself for whatever comes next.

ENVISION BETTER DAYS

by Peter Colwell

When you find yourself pining for a silver lining
But can only see that dark cloud ...
Take stock of what's working,
Not the dangers out lurking,
And speak these bold words loud and proud ...

"Better days are ahead for my family and me.
This I declare with certainty!
My confidence comes from unshaken belief
that God's on our side and will soon send relief."

It's a matter of time until things turn around
Until that day comes, keep your feet on the ground

Connect with the Earth and all of its beauty
Help those in need—it's our call to duty!

Life is a series of valleys and peaks
Peaks can last days ... and valleys last weeks
Use this time wisely and patiently wait
Preparing yourself for a life that is great!

3

KEY TAKEAWAYS
from Chapter Three

1. Identify negative behavior (yours or that of others) that is bringing you down and guard your integrity at all times.

2. Starve negative people of their power by refusing to fuel their negative agenda.

3. Ride the valleys and peaks of life with mindfulness and appreciation.

Goodbye, Worries!

by Peter Colwell

Worries can vanish at least for a while
And positive images stick
If we take the advice that has worked for so many:
"Do something for somebody, quick!"

When burdened with thoughts of defeat or despair
Turn from your troubles; show someone you care.
Time spent with others involved with their needs
Is an excellent way to begin sowing seeds.

The kind that will sprout …
And wash away doubt …
Giving us clues to what life's all about.

We're all in the same proverbial boat
Hustling like crazy to stay afloat.
Wondering when life will get back on a keel
That's even and steady, and not so surreal.

Let us pause for a moment, look up in the sky
And instead of asking ourselves "how?" and "why?"
Give thanks for the pleasure that comes from our giving.
That's when we'll discover the real joy of living!

chapter four

Grow from Your Experiences

Oh yes, the past can hurt. But the way I see it,
you can either run from it or learn from it.
RAFIKI (FROM DISNEY'S *THE LION KING*)

If you've ever been in a dead-end job with no chance for advancement; or worked in an unfriendly environment; or stayed in a personal relationship with an incompatible partner, hoping against hope it would all work out, you may feel like you threw away months or even years of your life that you can never get back. You might even harbor a sense of guilt or regret and think to yourself: *"Why did I waste so much time spinning my wheels and putting up with less than I deserve?"*

But there's good news for you to consider (ready for a silver lining?): There's no such thing as wasted time. You can—and do—grow from everything you experience. With the right frame of mind—and with the benefit of hindsight, which helps us look back on our experiences more clearly—we can extract the lessons from our difficult experiences and let go of the hurt.

Leave the pain in the past. Keep the lessons, on the other hand, in the forefront of your mind; let them spur you on to growth and help you make more informed decisions in the future. Benjamin Franklin, who constantly worked to improve himself, wrote:

"Those things that hurt, instruct." Experience can be your teacher, your guide, your way forward to a better, brighter life.

And remember: We grow not only from our own experiences but also the experiences of others, as well as the experiences we share with others. We can thus shorten our learning curves by taking lessons from other people's successes and setbacks. We can read biographies and memoirs to discover what the subjects of the books have discovered. We can also form mastermind groups, accelerating our growth by meeting with like-minded people who have similar—or, better yet, different!—pursuits.

THE WINDS OF CHANGE

by Peter Colwell

When the winds of change come blowing ...
That's the time to keep on showing
Our patient side
Don't let it hide
Keep learning and keep growing!

Learn, grow, develop. Rinse and repeat!
Don't stop until your journey's complete.
Savor the moment. See yourself winning!
What seems like the end ... may be a new beginning!

Ready or not, change is in the air.
Some change is fun, and some is not fair.
How we react will decide our course.
Which of our values will we enforce?

Choose to be steady and go with the flow.
Release all your worries. Let your confidence glow!
Shake off beliefs that no longer serve you.
Welcome a life that truly deserves you!

Life is for the living. Live it to the max.
Don't get bogged down with figures and facts.
Lift yourself up. Embrace each new day.
Trusting that God will show you the way!

A Chance Encounter
Leads to a Friendship of Growth

One of my dear friends is a spirited adventurer, world traveler, and successful entrepreneur named Prashant Koirala.

Prashant and I met in 2001 on, of all places, a bus. He was finishing up his studies at the University of Maryland and was working at a local convenience store near the apartment complex where I lived. I was sitting on the bus with my briefcase open and a copy of the manuscript for a motivational book I'd been writing on nights and weekends entitled *Spell SUCCESS in Your Life: A Road Map for Achieving Your Goals and Surviving Success* (Dreams Unlimited Press, 2002).

Prashant and I immediately struck up a conversation, and he took an active interest in the material I was writing—about goal setting, self-awareness, positive visualization, and creating a plan of action to achieve the desires of your heart.

As the bus approached his stop, we quickly exchanged our contact information, and Prashant wished me well on the book. Following my instincts, I handed him a copy of my valued manuscript and asked him to give me some feedback, hoping he would enjoy the read.

That chance encounter on the bus has led to a rich, fruitful friendship of growth that has lasted more than twenty years!

Growing a Business ... and Then Another ...

Initially, Prashant would simply e-mail me every once in a while— to say hello; to update me on his progress toward his goals; and to ask about my journey as a new dad, author, and speaker. But our friendship really deepened and solidified when we decided a few years later to form a mastermind group, so that we could actively and consistently help each other learn, grow, and develop by offering each other:

- Built-in accountability from our ongoing conversations.
- Idea sharing.
- Mutual encouragement.
- Celebration of successes.

When my daughter, Vanessa, was born, Prashant was the natural pick to be her godfather. He remains, even from a distance, a cherished part of our family.

Growing up in a small mountain region in the South Asian country of Nepal, Prashant began his informal entrepreneurial journey when he came to the United States, by himself, to pursue his education when he had just turned eighteen. Prashant thinks of an entrepreneur as being "a pursuer of opportunities independent of resources presently controlled." He's constantly been seeking entrepreneurial paths (since he had to put himself through college), and thus he's been involved in setting up numerous ventures—finding needs and filling them.

At first, he took on mini projects, like home tutoring to help students with math and science, and writing business plans for chefs and cooks who were starting ethnic restaurants. Eventually, Prashant got his first semi-structured exposure to business: He volunteered with Brian Cunningham, a successful entrepreneur (and his eventual mentor), to help inner-city entrepreneurs in Washington, DC, who were living at or below the poverty line start their own businesses.

Prashant was instantly able to connect with his clients, as he knew firsthand what it was like to begin from ground zero. Participants in Prashant's program were people who had previously run into problems with the law, and who now wanted to launch a more meaningful life. Prashant's program received support from many businesses in the inner city, and from several institutions as well.

Prashant graduated from the University of Maryland, at the top of his class, and started a career in private equity and venture capital to understand high-growth technology businesses. He also worked in an international investment bank, so that he could learn about transactions and expose himself to several emerging markets, including China and India.

For personal reasons, as well as his desire to have an adventure, Prashant next took an entrepreneurial role in a family fund to lead a healthcare company in India. He was attracted to the noble cause of treating people with sleep disorders, which were becoming chronic among professionals.

Even though he grew up in Nepal, Prashant says his experience running a venture in India was totally different. To build the business, he had to learn and adapt to India's ways. He and his team ultimately took the healthcare enterprise (Sleepcare) from a mere concept to a leading center in India for treating people with sleep issues.

After leaving his role with Sleepcare, Prashant decided to pursue his own path: to build a new-age university (Venturesity) that would disrupt how employers recruit new talent.

Prashant collaboratively acquired an online job board and began developing a network of recruiting-industry professionals. He started with the premise of building a talent pool for India's burgeoning technology industry; billions of dollars were pouring into these startups, thanks to both multinational companies and venture capitalists.

Prashant and his colleagues progressed with several business models before eventually discovering "hackathons" (real-world challenges that job seekers take on) as an innovative way to help organizations discover talent. It took a long time for the company to find the product-market fit, Prashant says. But once it did, it started growing at a rate of 200 percent month to month.

Prashant raised venture financing and had marquee technology companies like Amazon and Microsoft as clients, along with many high-growth startups. The rapid ascent, though, led to *growing pains*. The abundant capital they had available to them tempted the founding team to go in too many directions; they tried creating several businesses within the same business.

A Scare—and Then a New Direction

At the same time, Prashant and his beloved wife, Dixya, were becoming first-time parents. Unfortunately, Dixya had a difficult pregnancy. She developed a chronic condition called *Autoimmune Hemolytic Anemia*, a rare disorder characterized by the immune system attacking the body's own red blood cells. Dixya's doctors even discussed the possibility that the pregnancy might need to be terminated.

Prashant and Dixya were shattered. But Dixya stood determined, and Prashant stood with her. In the end, even with all the challenges they faced, Dixya and Prashant were blessed with a baby girl, Siya.

By then, the company Prashant had co-founded had gone in yet another direction. He felt it would be best run by his partners and a new set of institutional investors.

At the time, Prashant struggled with the decision both personally and professionally. He knew—from articles, books, and the stories of others—that business is always up and down. But it's a slightly different curveball when you're at the cross-section of both personal and professional challenges. You need courage of your own, of course; but more importantly, you need the support of an ecosystem of well-meaning friends and family to carry you through.

You don't build that ecosystem overnight; it's a continuous part of your journey.

Prashant eventually decided to take on another role: to "solve a problem for a billion," using a compelling technology to drive scale. That journey continues today, and Prashant is evolving through his experiences. He's still learning, for example, that when you're an entrepreneur, there is no separation between your personal life and building a business; it all converges.

He's also living through the highs and the lows, financial and emotional. During the highs, cash is flowing and business is booming. During the lows—well, it used to be that Prashant felt like the world was coming to an end during the lows. But slowly, he has become more resilient and has developed more tolerance for the ambiguity. He has not only grown ecosystems and networks; he has also grown a thick(er) skin to deal with the inevitable issues that come up each day.

When you're an entrepreneur, Prashant says, you have to remain grounded and rooted, even—especially—when you're surrounded by problems (which is every day!). But solving those problems, Prashant stresses—relying on your previous experiences—gives you the tools you need to ... solve additional problems. It's humbling, but it's also rewarding. As Shakespeare said: "Joy's soul lies in the doing."

Prashant has been an entrepreneur for fifteen years now. He has never had "the same repeat day." Each new day, in fact, brings its own joys and sorrows, he says.

And he believes we're all best served by embracing both.

The whole universe is change,
and life itself is but what you deem it.
MARCUS AURELIUS
(Note: This is one of Prashant's favorite mantras.)

LEADING WITH STRENGTH
by Peter Colwell

Your strength as a leader will often depend
On what kind of message you're willing to send.
At first sign of trouble, will you break? Will you bend?
Stay true to your values right to the end?

Will you lead with your heart
And not just your head?
First the horse, THEN the cart ...
Will you lead ... or be led?

At the end of the day, a leader must *care.*
A leader must *do* and a leader must *dare.*
A leader must *learn* and a leader must *share.*
For knowledge is nothing until we give it away,
Empowering others to *seize the day*!

Each moment presents us with chances anew
To draw forth in others the BEST they can do!

"Growth Is Not Automatic"

As success coach Dave Martin often says: "Growth is not automatic. It is your responsibility." We don't just push a button and grow. We need to take action, regularly, to make it happen.

Laurie Snyder, a graduate of a leadership program I conducted, realizes that change is inevitable, both for organizations and for us as people. You have to expect it and be ready to pivot when you need to, she says. If you don't, you get left behind.

Laurie has learned to embrace change and show confidence regardless of outward circumstances. She exerts her own leadership by being a positive influence on any team she works on.

Having seen other leaders come and go from positions, she says one principle rings true for her: ***Real* leaders fall down and get back up again.** They accept a challenge and embrace the role. They listen to their team. They learn, from poor leaders, what not to do and then do the opposite.

Wannabe leaders, on the other hand, say—or imply: **I'm the boss. Do what I say.**

Laurie has built her strength by facing challenges, overcoming temporary hard knocks and bad breaks along the way. She says the difficult times have taught her two crucial lessons about experiences and growth:

- You can't bank on anything. So be grateful for the times when you *are* in a good place personally and professionally.

- You can put your experience to good use now by applying what you've learned from it to a new situation.

CALM IN THE STORM

by Peter Colwell

In a world where fear and stress are the norm
Now more than ever, be a calm in the storm.
Placid and tranquil, peaceful, serene ...
These are the thoughts on which we must lean.

Tumultuous times require our best.
When positive thoughts are put to the test.
Confident action will help us reveal
a strength from within that no one can steal.

Swirling around us is chaos unfurled
hurling us into an uncertain world.

When nothing seems normal, we may yearn for the past.
Hoping our memories of good times will last.

Instead, let us face this new frontier
with courage and calmness, and a healthy fear.

One that engages our innovation
giving us bursts of inspiration
guiding us toward a new creation ...
A world of compassion and appreciation!

"The Show Must Go On!"

If ever there were a master of growing from your experiences, it would be my long-time friend Brian Kelly. I was introduced to Brian by a mutual acquaintance, and our bond has lasted nearly two decades and counting. Through the years, we have communicated with each other to promote each other's brands, road-test each other's advice and products, and, most importantly, encourage each other's growth and happiness.

Brian is an entrepreneur whose primary focus is to make a difference in people's lives and help them as much as possible—specifically, in his case, by creating products and services for clients in the wellness industry. His secondary focus is making money.

When Brian started his journey in 2009 at Babson College, he was gung-ho about physical fitness; the broader concept of wellness was not as embedded in society at that time. Soon, though, Brian expanded from fitness to helping people be more holistically well and improve their mental, emotional, and physical well-being.

Brian is a partner at FIT Company, a corporate wellness firm whose main offering (The FIT Company Challenge) is putting on fitness/wellness events for client companies' employees. Brian and his leadership team focus on running in-person challenges all over America (Washington, DC; Boston; Nashville; San Diego; and Chicago being just a few of the cities they've visited), with their biggest events in Texas (Houston, Austin, Dallas). Office teams train for the event and go through a series of challenges on the big day: for example, walk/run, relay, squats, push-ups, and inverted rows. FIT Company emphasizes the idea that completing the challenge is more important than winning it. Children and pets of the participants come out to cheer them on. Teams that didn't think they could win come from behind. Participants find the experience motivational and gratifying.

As is the case with many entrepreneurs, Brian and his team faced significant hurdles in launching their company, and they continue to deal with challenges in sustaining it; there are many potential reasons to throw in the towel and forget about the dream. What keeps Brian going, he says, is remembering the moments when he and his team have made a difference at his events. He regularly hears from participants who talk about changing their attitudes, having more fun, and investing in their own well-being—all of which fuels Brian and his colleagues to keep doing what they do.

It's mentally challenging to not only run corporate events with six-figure budgets in multiple cities, but to bootstrap them as an entrepreneur—to pull off a "champagne event" with a "beer budget," as Brian puts it. That's one of just many reasons why Brian's mantra is: **"The show must go on!"**

Once, when Brian was in Chicago for one of his company's corporate fitness events, he woke up in the morning to a windy, freezing day. As a result, many of the firms that had signed up to participate in the activities had backed out. Moreover, half of the help had failed to show up.

Brian and his business partner wondered whether it was worth continuing for just a small group of people under harsh conditions, especially for an event that would not make a profit under the circumstances. But Brian stuck to his philosophy—"the show must go on!"—and he was determined to give everyone the best experience possible.

The participants who showed up got drenched but had an extraordinary day of fun. It would have been so easy to cancel on them, Brian says. But because the show went on, it became one of the most memorable events of Brian's career.

The Bear Encounter

At 6:30 on a beautiful June morning, my wife, Trevia, and I woke up to the sound of a visitor to our campsite—a visitor that was about four feet tall and weighed a few hundred pounds.

A black bear was rumbling and thudding around, knocking over our ice cooler, which had our drinks in it.

Trevia peered out the screen of the tent and whispered a play-by-play of what was happening. Eventually the bear came within about two feet of us—at the front end of our tent—and made a hole in the netting of the clubhouse next to us, where we had stored our food in sealed containers. The bear then grabbed a Ziploc bag in her teeth and walked twenty feet away to feast on her newfound breakfast: our daughter Vanessa's baby food.

Trevia and I were up on our feet inside the tent, so we could see the bear devouring her bounty. Let's just say the experience was ... unnerving! In fact, another group of campers just down the road from us saw the whole thing and stood frozen in their tracks, watching the bear's every move.

Fortunately, Vanessa and our son, Petey, were asleep the whole time.

The bear made quick work of the food she had taken. She then ... proceeded back toward our tent, presumably for more food.

Moment of truth!

Luckily, I had a whistle with me in the tent. I'd brought it in case we should encounter a bear, which I never in a million years dreamed would actually happen!

As the bear approached to within ten feet of us, I blew the whistle as loudly as I could. She stopped in her tracks, startled ... then took another step forward.

So I blew the whistle ten or fifteen more times. And finally, the bear retreated out of our campsite—and kept going.

Once the coast was clear, Trevia and I swept the kids out of the tent and into our minivan, just to play it safe. We then looked up and saw the bear at the top of a hill—walking away with her three cubs in tow.

With our adrenaline running high—and grateful to be alive!—we cut our trip short a night early. We'd been camping for four nights, so we'd already gotten our money's worth. We didn't want to take any chances on a return visit that night or the next morning, especially since the bear knew we had food.

Trevia was so dazed by what had happened that she drove us home in the wrong direction. I was equally dazed and didn't notice. So what should have been a three-hour trip took us seven hours. We got a scenic tour of West Virginia, though!

Encountering that bear was, without question, the scariest moment of our lives. On the one hand, we were fascinated; on the other, we were terrified. Luckily, we were (mostly) able to keep our composure and use the resources we had available—in this case, a whistle—to escape.

What's really interesting, though, as I look back on the experience now, is that I grew from it. All of us did.

For me personally: One major benefit of confronting my fear head-on (as if we had the option to run!) and living to tell the story is that I now have a renewed sense of confidence that I can handle any challenge life throws my way. I also have greater appreciation for how precious life is, so I'm far less likely to put off the things I really want to do.

Trevia, by the way, later bought me a small, plastic black bear that I now have on my desk at work. Whenever I'm up against a big problem, I picture myself just inches away from the actual bear—which quickly puts things back into perspective.

What challenges are you facing in your life right now? How can you turn a seemingly negative experience into a positive one by finding the ways you can grow from it?

____

____

____

What are you scared of? Rejection or disapproval? Other people's opinions of you? Falling short of others' expectations? Making a fool of yourself? Too much responsibility? Asking for what you want?

____

____

____

Overcoming our fear of something gives us confidence that we can confront other fears and meet them head-on. Success breeds success. Confidence in one area of your life can lead to confidence in many areas of your life.

Sometimes, life will bombard you with a series of frustrating setbacks: a layoff at work, a rejection letter from a prospective employer, a voicemail or text from a love interest explaining why "something has suddenly come up," a financial ledger with a negative net income.

Whatever difficulties you face, and regardless of the number, you can find a way around them. When your dream seems stuck or blocked, your best chance for success is to create your own window of opportunity—to use your experience as a catalyst to grow and to meet the moment.

> *Pain nourishes courage. You can't be brave if you've*
> *only had wonderful things happen to you.*
> MARY TYLER MOORE

Growing from Experience—Together

Some of the best growth experiences are the ones we don't see coming. Since we don't plan them, we have no idea what they'll be (or how they'll turn out) until we take action.

I was once part of a mentoring program at a Fortune 500 company where I had risen in the ranks over a decade and a half. I was selected to be the mentor to an up-and-coming manager in northern California named Jason Smith.

The pairing was a match made in heaven. Jason and I met in Dallas for the kickoff event and then embarked on a ten-month program of biweekly phone calls and coaching. We also visited each other in person: Jason came to Washington, DC, where I played host; and I went to San Francisco, where Jason showed me around his offices and the beautiful City by the Bay.

The mentoring program reached its crescendo with a gathering back in Dallas in late 2018. There, the mentor-protégé teams got to celebrate the relationships that had been formed, the lessons learned, and the wisdom we would all take with us into the future.

Years after the program ended, my connection with Jason (and vice versa!) is as strong as ever. We help each other navigate career shifts and related challenges.

"You're Going to Hit a Few Walls ..."

Jason grew up in southern California, and he was interested in real estate from a young age. He was always impressed with big houses. In fact, he wanted to live in one someday.

Jason studied business administration in college and jumped into the real estate field as a loan officer and as a mortgage broker before moving into property management. He enjoyed being a loan officer in particular because he's always been drawn to financing and putting deals together. It's exciting, he says—the thrill of the chase! Making deals materialize transferred nicely to the field of property management, giving Jason the chance to build a foundation of what he would continue to attract and pursue.

You have to try a few things as you start out in your career, Jason emphasizes. **You're going to hit a few walls before you find out what works or what sticks**.

In college, Jason was relatively shy and unassuming. His uncle, a successful business owner, recommended that Jason's first job out of college be in ... sales, even though it was far from what Jason saw himself doing. It was a way out of his comfort zone, though. And as Neale Donald Walsch points out: "Life begins at the end of your comfort zone."

Jason agreed to give sales a try. His uncle had him sell smog machines to local gas stations for vehicle testing. It was Jason's first "real job." He would visit gas stations in northern California and see if they wanted to buy a smog tester. The process was awkward and challenging. Jason sold two testers in six months; his goal was to sell two *per month*.

Before long, Jason realized that he had to switch to a job that would give him a more reliable income; the commission-only model didn't fit him. But it did teach him a few things.

During that bleak period of two sales in six months, Jason learned about persistence. He also learned the fundamentals of the sales cycle, and to admire people in sales and what they do each day. Take cold calling, for example. Jason hates it, and he does very little of it himself. But thanks to his experience working for his uncle, he does have an *appreciation* for it.

Jason says the most important question we need to ask ourselves is: *"What fits me?"* You don't want to continue down a path that's not natural for you, one that makes you feel unsettled *all* the time. A *little* unease is fine and natural. But *continuous* discomfort likely signals a bad fit, or at the very least a need for more training that will help you refine your skills and be more successful.

When it comes to growing from your experiences, think of yourself as a plant, Jason suggests: If you're not in the right environment, one where you excel, then your growth will be significantly hindered.

Jason still remembers a piece of crucial advice he got in his twenties: **"Put your seedling where you can grow the most."** Have the self-awareness to acknowledge the truth if you're not where you belong right now. Yes, you will grow through your experiences. But why stay for the long term in a situation where you're not going to prosper?

Dealing with—and Learning from—Difficulties

My pairing with Jason Smith has been phenomenal in that our core values (continuous development, leadership, public speaking, positive thinking, and reflection) are closely aligned. We share an excitement to learn as much as we can from our experiences and then get out there on the megaphone and let other people know!

Jason eventually had the opportunity to replicate on the West Coast a leadership program I had started with colleagues on the East Coast. He was given tools and templates for the job, but it was clear he'd have to breathe life into the program. He was responsible for a production, and he took that responsibility seriously. It was a leap of faith for him, one that allowed him to stretch himself and grow as a leader of leaders.

Jason ultimately succeeded by shifting his mindset away from himself and onto the participants in his program; it was all about *them* and *their* development, he realized. By focusing outward instead of inward, he took the pressure off himself and instead channeled everything he'd learned from his own experiences toward the program participants.

And that's when he came alive!

It's been especially rewarding, he says, to help junior leaders build their confidence. It allows Jason to pay his blessings forward to them, share his values with them, and participate in their growth.

When something difficult comes down the pike (often unexpected), Jason has some go-to responses that guide him through it:

- **Understand the *real* situation** behind high emotions, and discover what's happening under the surface. Find the most logical way to respond—and take emotion out of that response.

- **Take time to breathe** in the moment, or step away from the situation if you need to. That way you'll be calm when you get back to the problem.

- **Match energy with the other people in the situation** to build rapport with them. Jump in their shoes and realize that they might simply be having a bad day; what's happening may have nothing to do with you.

- **Make sure that love and tolerance are in the forefront**, and seek agreement as soon as possible to de-escalate the situation. Try to find common ground to solve a problem or take a first step toward resolution.

When things are very hard, Jason likes to write down what's weighing on him (or what he'd like to eventually address). He then puts the item(s) in a shoebox in his closet and waits until he's strong enough to "climb that mountain." He sets small goals and tries to be extra kind to himself so that he gets back to a better place.

His advice on growing from your experiences:

- **You're at where you're at for a reason.** Control what you can, and always be pursuing a better version of yourself. Be patient, but accelerate when opportunities present themselves.

- **Don't tolerate a bad situation.** If it's not working, it's not likely to get better just because it looks good on paper.

- **Don't give up too soon.** Hold on until the tide begins to turn in your favor.

- **Be ready for what the world gives you.** It may not be what you want, but it's usually what you need. And you will always learn something from it.

GOD STILL HAS YOUR BACK

by Peter Colwell

In moments of trial, it all becomes clear ...
We suddenly focus on what we hold dear.
Our major concerns from previous days
Slowly but surely get lost in the haze.

What once was important (or so we had thought)
Gives way to a purpose we'd never sought.

A brand-new challenge to test our resilience
A puzzle whose answer will require our brilliance.

Putting our minds together as one
Preparing ourselves for a fight well won

In the midst of a dark and turbulent time
Don't lose sight of a gift so sublime
A God who sheds eternal light
And has our back throughout this plight

Whose faith expands when ours recedes
Who always knows our greatest needs
Who lifts us up when all else fails
Whose everlasting love prevails

3

KEY TAKEAWAYS
from Chapter Four

1. Learn, grow, develop. Rinse and repeat.
   Don't stop until your journey is complete.

2. Relying on our previous experiences
   helps us solve new problems.

3. You're going to hit a few walls before
   you discover what works.

Grace Overflowing
by Peter Colwell

The dizzying pace our world has required
Can leave us weary, worn out, and tired.
But grace under pressure can help us perform
Adapting, adjusting to a brand-new norm.

When faced with a loss that cannot be surmounted,
All of our blessings must then be counted.
Giving us space to reinvent …
Granting us grace to circumvent
Patterns of old that no longer serve …
Inviting a life we truly deserve!

Earthly angels will appear
On the other side of fear.
Broken hearts will one day mend
God's gracious love will never end!

chapter five

Elevate Your Expectations

*Whether you think you can
or you think you can't—you're right.*

HENRY FORD

In the hit romantic comedy *Sleepless in Seattle*, actors Meg Ryan and Bill Pullman play an engaged couple named Annie and Walter who have become distant from each other in recent months. In fact, Annie has been falling in love, from afar in New York City, with someone whose voice she heard on a radio call-in show—a man in Seattle who had recently lost his wife.

On Valentine's Day, Annie struggles to end her relationship with Walter over dinner at an elegant New York restaurant. She tells him that the man she has feelings for, who she hasn't yet met, might be waiting for her at that moment atop the Empire State Building, where they had planned (albeit very ambiguously!) to meet that night.

When Annie looks over and sees a large heart lighting up on the side of the building, she knows it's a sign. So she listens to her own heart and ends her relationship with Walter.

Walter's enlightened response: "Marriage is hard enough without bringing such low expectations into it."

Our lives are filled with challenges, and we have to decide what our expectations are (or will be). If we set our sights too low, we may avoid disappointment; but we might also miss out on the amazing opportunities life has to offer. You might go to a "safety school," for example, instead of challenging yourself academically. You might take a job that doesn't require you to stretch and grow. You might decide not to try out for a part in the play. You might stay put instead of moving to a more desirable location.

Take a chance! All life is a chance. The [person] who goes farthest is generally the one who is willing to do and dare.
DALE CARNEGIE

Why not elevate your expectations instead?

Elevating your expectations is not about being more *than* who you are. It's about being more *of* who you are. It's about defining the standards by which you will live your life, relate with others, and do business.

"Don't Forget About Your Dream!"

Sadly, most of us are not living up to our potential; we are not coming close to achieving what we're capable of.

What if the primary reason behind this tragedy is not lack of money or lack of desire or lack of will but, rather, lack of courage? Many of us are simply afraid to take the next step or move up to the next level in life. Doing so might require more responsibility, we think to ourselves, or expose our flaws to others.

Maybe you have a deep-seated fear of failing—or an even deeper fear of succeeding. Imagine that you're coasting along in a job, one that you've mastered but that no longer challenges or fulfills you. Then, one day, you realize that other people you know are out there living *your* dream, following *your* star, playing out what could be the story book of *your* life. At that point, might you start second-guessing yourself?

One of the best pieces of advice I ever got came from a colleague of mine who knew about my passion for speaking and my goal of one day making an income from it. As I told her about some of my other interests and activities, she responded with words I'll always remember: "Those things you're doing are great, but don't forget about your dream!"

Wow. Her words rang in my ears like a clashing symbol:

Don't forget about your dream!

We often allow ourselves to get sidetracked or derailed in life. We're scared of what might happen if we were to actually follow through and pursue our dreams. Author Susan Jeffers offers this gutsy response: "Feel the fear and do it anyway."

Set Long-Range Goals

You can start, today, by setting some long-range goals—the kind of goals that will be "ready to hatch" at least ten years from now. Achieving these goals will require energy, patience, and the cultivation of habits and attitudes that will help bring your aspirations to fruition. Long-range goals help us overcome short-term challenges along the way. In fact, you should write down more goals than you can possibly accomplish in your lifetime. That way you'll have a virtually endless supply of them to draw upon as your life changes direction and your relationships evolve.

To set long-range goals, you need to have a flexible mind and a creative attitude. Think about when we were children. We said:

"When I grow up, I want to be a ___________."

While most of us didn't give ourselves a deadline for achieving our childhood dreams, we were definitely looking then at goals that would take ten, twenty, or more years to materialize.

Now is your chance to put a rough deadline on those goals, whether they include retirement planning, vacation destinations, or career milestones. By spelling out your long-term goals and writing them down, you will be taking a definitive step toward your dreams that most people *never* take. You'll be putting your vision into print.

Author Brian Tracy says that 95 percent of people never write down their goals. Then they wonder why they've missed out on opportunities to advance in their careers, make more money, or become healthier and happier.

In the Short Term, Focus on Focus

Dashed dreams and missed opportunities over the long haul are often the result of a lack of focus in our daily lives. More often than not, we can achieve our long-range goals if we *focus* our efforts day to day, week to week, month to month.

Doctors and scientists are just two examples of professionals who harness focus in their careers. They work in the short term to discover and implement new ways to improve the human condition. But their activities are always connected to the longer-term goal of achieving medical or scientific breakthroughs.

We should all take this same approach: We should all live a focused, purpose-driven life that has clear goals and expectations.

Shooting in too many directions at once diminishes our chances of being effective in any of those directions. So instead of trying to accomplish, say, fifteen goals this year, why not direct your mental and emotional energy toward one or two that will make the greatest difference in your life? Decide what your *top* objectives are, both personally and professionally, and then commit yourself to making *those* things happen in the short term.

I tested this approach firsthand one year, giving myself only two major professional goals: 1) to publish my first book; and 2) to become a part-time paid professional speaker. Starting January 1, I focused on only those two tasks.

What happened? By the end of the year, I had achieved both goals. In fact, the two dreams came true within a month of each other!

You can get help staying focused by telling a trusted group of friends and colleagues about your plans. Ask them to hold you accountable and offer gentle reminders throughout the year.

You can also stay focused on your short-term goals by displaying them in several places: in your day planner, on your refrigerator door, inside your most frequently used desk drawer, or in your purse or briefcase. These reminder notes will act as subtle motivators to keep you on track and determined to succeed.

Concentrate all your thoughts upon the work at hand.
The sun's rays do not burn until brought to a focus.
ALEXANDER GRAHAM BELL

Expect—and Be Willing— to Change Direction

To succeed in whatever we do, we must be willing to change direction. In fact, we need to expect it.

Yes, we should have a map (i.e., goals and plans) to guide us; but we also need to be able to throw away the compass and make strategic revisions when necessary, often on the fly—because life circumstances throw all of us in directions we never thought possible.

Take, for example, the recall of California Governor Gray Davis in 2003, which propelled actor and bodybuilder Arnold Schwarzenegger into the political arena—and right into the California governor's seat as Davis's replacement. We hear of product recalls all the time, but it isn't every day that an elected official gets recalled.

After a whirlwind campaign, Schwarzenegger was elected to the most powerful position in one of America's most influential states. His willingness to change course gave him a once-in-a-lifetime opportunity to serve his state and country in a way he never could have done as an actor or a bodybuilder.

Do Something Immediately to Build Momentum

Right after I set the goal of becoming a part-time paid professional speaker, I searched the Internet for organizations looking for speakers. I followed up by contacting the appropriate people associated with the groups.

Within a week, I received some replies. And a couple of months later, I was booked to address a local association.

My free presentation that evening led to my first paid speaking engagement: a keynote address at a local college. Then the ripple effect took hold, and each subsequent presentation led to additional paid speaking opportunities. I had spurred momentum by simply contacting the right people and following up.

That same year, I had also vowed to see my first book go to print. The printing itself, of course, would cost money—and I needed to generate some. So I sent fliers to family and friends, offering them a pre-release special price if they ordered my book in advance of publication.

The campaign successfully covered my printing costs. And four months later, my book was in readers' hands.

Be a Light to Others

I first met Tyler Merrill in the hallway of his church, where both of our sons attended Scout meetings. The two of us quickly struck up a fun conversation, and we enjoyed each other's positive spirit.

Several months later, we unexpectedly ran into each other at a regional real estate association event. "What are you doing here?" we both joyfully blurted out at the same time. Neither of us had any idea that we worked in the same industry. Tyler was a business developer for a janitorial company that services buildings run by property management firms. I was a regional director of property management operations for a global real estate services firm.

But our commonalities didn't stop there.

We soon realized that we also shared an affinity for the human relations principles taught by Dale Carnegie, and that we had both graduated from the "Dale Carnegie Course in Effective Communication and Human Relations" that has been around for more than a century. (In fact, Tyler eventually became my graduate assistant for the first Dale Carnegie Course I facilitated as a newly certified instructor.)

Though I thought I couldn't possibly have anything else in common with Tyler, our worlds converged yet again when I co-led new-hire onboarding seminars at work; Tyler offered to sponsor lunch for the events and to give a short, inspirational keynote speech called "Being a Light to Others."

One of Tyler's admirable qualities is that he adds value to any conversation he's a part of with his intent listening skills and his desire to redirect situations toward the positive. He routinely creates upswings, in thought and action, among everyone he encounters. You leave an interaction with Tyler feeling uplifted and ready to win the day (or enjoy the evening)!

Putting Other People First

Tyler grew up in a small town in Oregon. He says he was aware of only a few jobs when he was young: doctor, lawyer, post office worker, teacher, and coach. To him, there weren't many other career paths outside of that handful.

Tyler always knew he wanted to interact closely with people in whatever he ultimately decided to do with his life. A church leader counseled him early on that his greatest satisfaction would come when he served others. That conversation stuck, and from then on Tyler was determined to weave service into his career.

He took a job right out of college at the bottom of the 2008-2009 economic recession. At the time, there were few career possibilities out there. So, quite ironically, he accepted a training position with hospital staff in Austin, Texas—even though he'd sworn he would never work in a hospital, since he faints at the sight of blood.

But as the primary breadwinner in his family (which at the time included a new son), Tyler didn't have the luxury of waiting for options. Moreover, he's always believed in putting other people first. So he took the opportunity that was in front of him and grew where he was planted, working continuously to learn, develop, and improve.

Those early experiences have served as the building blocks of Tyler's career.

Opportunities and people—far richer and broader than he could have imagined—have come into his life and enriched it. Indeed, he's always known that he can't attain personal and career success on his own. So he relies on a team of people around him to achieve results. Calculated risks have propelled him to a place where failure (if it happens) isn't catastrophic; it just becomes a learning tool for his next venture.

While ambition is admirable and drives us forward, Tyler remains rooted in his family responsibilities, putting his role as husband and father first. As David O. McKay says: "No worldly success can compensate for failure in the home." It doesn't matter how successful you are outside the home if you're unsuccessful in the home. That's why Tyler has structured his career so that he can be in a position of influence without being pulled away from his

No. 1 role in life: father. Jobs come and go. Currency flows. But kids are eternal.

Tyler tests himself frequently by asking himself the question: *"How do my wife and kids feel about me?"* His goals are to love, nurture, teach, and engage. He is constantly and happily balancing work and family—being true to who he is based on past decisions that have formed his path.

Tyler's larger-than-life enthusiasm comes from his deep desire to be the light he wants to see in the world. He models friendliness. He waves and smiles because he wants to see joy around him. He expects adventure and amazement, challenges and change. He refuses to play life safe.

And he hopes you'll approach *your* life the same way, relying on your own great expectations as well as the people around you. In his words:

"Don't feel like the entire success or failure is 100 percent on your shoulders. You need other people to make your dreams and desires pay off. It's not all on you. But you do need to put in 110 percent effort. Work like it's all up to you, but pray like it's all up to God. Go forward with faith—hoping, praying, and desiring that it will all work out!"

BE THE LIGHT

by Peter Colwell

A world that's often void of light
Bereft of joy and full of plight
Can make the best of us lose sight
Of what it takes to win the fight.

And yet we all possess within
Capacity to "rein it in"

To muster up our inner strength
To travel to the greatest length …

Beyond what first we could conceive
Made possible when we believe …
Empowered by Divinity
And human creativity

Be the light you wish to see
To benefit posterity
A light that shines so bright and free
From hither to eternity!

Be Easy to Work With

If you want to influence people, move up in your career, or simply get more of what you want out of life, be easy to work with. Make things simple for people. Don't complicate things.

If you're in a service industry especially—which most of us are, effectively—keep your customers and clients happy (or at least try to resolve their problems). Find out what their needs and concerns are, then follow up with solutions as quickly as you can.

One of the best compliments you can get from someone is: *"You're so easy to work with."* When someone likes dealing with you, you're likely to get repeat business and/or referrals from them recommending your products or services. So don't make people struggle; find the path of least resistance. Make transactions enjoyable and memorable. Surprise people by delivering more than you promised—on time (or before!).

The same "be easy to work with" principle applies to our personal relationships. Who are *you* more likely to spend time with—people who are easygoing and happy-go-lucky; or people who take life too seriously, complain constantly, and complicate even the simplest of matters?

If you're a supervisor, you will be seen as a rare treasure if you simply present yourself as approachable. So have an open-door policy. Develop the attitude that no question is "dumb." Offer your employees encouragement and support, and don't forget to praise them for a job well done. As Jess Lair, author of *I Ain't Much, Baby—but I'm All I've Got!* notes: "Praise is like sunlight to the warm human spirit; we cannot flower and grow without it." Novelist Charles Dickens once said that a sincere compliment would have him "floating on clouds" for months.

A Little Caring Goes a Long Way

When I was in my early twenties, I took a job as a concierge at a small hotel, where I learned the ropes of customer service.

One evening, I spent at least an hour with a retired couple from the Midwest—Mr. and Ms. McArdell—who had been visiting the Washington, DC, area for a week. They wanted to make several day trips, including an excursion a few states away.

To help them find their way, I pulled out an atlas (Note to young readers: For more information on what an atlas is, search the term on Google!) and mapped out the best route for them to take. I also gave them an alternate route they could use, in case the first one didn't work out.

I then wrote down for the couple a list of hotels and motels in the areas they'd be visiting, and I recommended some dining and entertainment options, too. I even researched special events the two of them could attend.

Ms. McArdell was impressed with the level of service and attention she and her husband got from me—so much so that she said to me something I remember to this day (I wrote it down at the time!):

> **You keep caring about people the**
> **way you do and you're gonna make it.**

If you simply show people that you genuinely care about them—by listening to their needs, responding to them, and going beyond what's normally expected—you'll not only feel great about yourself; you'll strengthen your relationships with others, too.

Strive for Significance

People often get caught up in the pursuit of material success. They go after more money, a bigger house, fancier cars, a more deluxe lifestyle.

But if we make material gain our sole objective in life, neglecting the opportunity to also make a difference in other people's lives, we will have nothing to show for ourselves at the end of our time on Earth.

So instead of striving solely for worldly success, strive for significance. Our primary aim in life should be, as Rabbi Harold Kushner puts it, to "live a life that matters."

Imagine what the world would be like if we could instill in the hearts and minds of our youth and adults that their lives really do matter—that life is not an accident, and that we all have a significant role to play in improving the world around us!

Don't limit investing to the financial world.
Invest something of yourself,
and you will be richly rewarded.
CHARLES SCHWAB

Leave a Legacy

Legendary comedian Bob Hope lived to be one hundred years old. His gifts to the world were his sharp wit, his spontaneous sense of humor, and his willingness and ability to lift people's spirits.

After touring vaudeville early in his career, Hope acted in more than fifty movies, performed on Broadway, graced the airwaves with his own radio show, and appeared in nearly three hundred TV specials over seven decades. He was most well-known for entertaining American troops worldwide during several wars and conflicts throughout the twentieth century.

Think about this, though: What if Hope had given up on his gifts, to instead find a "real job"? What if he had dismissed his own talents? The world would have missed out on one of the finest comedic talents ever.

But because he insisted on following his calling to entertain the world, Hope set sail on a path that earned him sixty-five honorary doctorates, several congressional awards, an honorary Oscar, and a spot in the *Guinness Book of World Records* for most awards received by an entertainer.

Hope left a legacy of laughter and goodwill, simply by being true to his purpose—and aligning his expectations with it!

SOARING TO NEW HEIGHTS

by Peter Colwell

Many of us have the impulse to soar
We are deeply inspired right down to our core
To dare and to dream ... to achieve so much more
Far beyond anything imagined before.

Greater than knowledge, more precious than wit
Is our will to conquer ... by way of true grit
Our passion for greatness and our desire to rise
Will all but ensure that we claim our prize.

The top of the mountain is there for the taking.
With action, our goals are dreams-in-the-making.
Set your sights high and don't hesitate.
You have to get started ... if you want to be great!

Go the Extra Mile

One sunny day in mid-June, my wife, Trevia, and I set out on a fifty-mile bike ride with our son, Petey, who needed to ride that distance in one day to complete his Cycling merit badge—a requirement for the rank of Eagle Scout.

We charted the course we intended to follow, reserving a cabin for the evening after we'd completed what we anticipated would be a strenuous day. We planned to ride along a portion of the Chesapeake & Ohio Canal, which runs along the Potomac River in the mid-Atlantic region of the United States.

Once we had our bikes, food, and gear ready, a friend dropped us off and encouraged us to "make good choices"—a loving maternal recommendation.

The first twenty miles of the trip went smoothly. We got into a good rhythm, took routine water and snack breaks, and savored our pace, the fresh air, and the beautiful weather.

Then things quickly changed: Dark clouds came over us, and the sky opened up with a downpour of rain accompanied by lightning and thunder.

Not So "Well"

At first, we celebrated this sudden shift in the atmosphere, as the rain was refreshingly cool. But before long, the cold reality of muddy, impassable trails began to set in, thwarting our efforts to reach our goal.

For a while, we resorted to walking our bikes through the puddles. Soon, though, even walking became treacherous. To make matters worse, we came to a detour sign directing us away from the trail; it was closed for repairs. We then had no choice but to ride (or try to!) steeply uphill, which again forced us at many points to simply walk instead.

After a while, we reached more-level ground, where we were able to get our bearings, follow the detour signs, and re-establish our groove. But as the day wore on, our water supply dwindled until we eventually ran out altogether. We asked a stranger for help, and he gladly invited us into his house so that we could load up on cold, fresh water to get us through the rest of our journey.

As early evening approached, we stopped at a tavern for a bite to eat. We told the waitress about our adventures up to that point, and she wished us well on the rest of our ride.

Unfortunately, things didn't go so "well."

At the forty-mile mark, we reached a point of peak exhaustion, our endurance flagging. We weren't sure we could continue, especially given the weight of our backpacks and gear. So we came to a consensus as a family—or so I thought—that we would not be able to finish the ride.

Then Trevia had an idea.

"Why don't you ask that man in the red shirt up the hill if he can drive me to the cabin at the campground where we'll be staying tonight, and if we can load most of our gear into his truck to free up the weight on your backs so that you two can hopefully finish the fifty miles before midnight?"

With nothing to lose, I walked onto the man's property. He was standing outside his truck, smoking a cigarette and staring at me with a scowl.

It was then that I noticed the "No Trespassing" sign I'd walked right past.

With my hands at my sides to show I was coming in peace, I told the man about our dilemma and asked if he would drive Trevia—and our stuff—ten miles away to the campground. Seconds seemed like minutes as I awaited his response. Finally, he put out his cigarette and said: "Sure. Give me a few minutes to bring the truck around."

So we loaded up the truck. And then, with a strange mix of relief and uncertainty, I kissed my wife goodbye as she drove off with a total stranger!

A Second Wind—and Then Confusion

With the weight removed from our backs and just water and sugary snacks to see us through, Petey and I headed forward, now re-invigorated and newly hopeful that we would reach our goal. But before long, the sky started to darken as the glimmers of light from the setting sun slowly disappeared.

Petey's phone battery had died. Mine had just 1 percent left.

We reached an unfamiliar stretch of land past a row of trees and thickets. We came to an intersection, and we had to decide whether to veer left slightly or make a hard right turn.

I called Trevia to a) make sure she was OK (she was), and b) see if she could point us in the right direction. But as I started to explain where we were, my phone died too.

Now, Petey and I would have to just roll the dice and decide— left, or right?

We chose right.

And that was wrong.

We didn't realize it, of course, until we had pedaled several miles in that fateful direction. Worse, there was no one in sight that we could reach out to for help or guidance.

Finally, though, we saw signs of civilian activity. We turned down a hill and came upon an establishment that was still open. We parked our bikes, looked up, and realized that we had stopped at ... the very same tavern where we had eaten earlier in the day.

By this time, we had ridden *more* than fifty miles, but we would have several more miles to go to reach the campground—and we had no clue how to get there (and very little energy left).

The Last Mile

The waitress inside the tavern—the same one who had served us previously—asked where Trevia was.

"Long story," I replied.

We then met two women who desperately wanted to help us. They weren't sure how they could manage it logistically. But soon enough, they came up with a solution—sort of.

One woman opened the trunk of her car and managed to squeeze both of our bikes in, sideways. The other woman fit Petey and me snugly into her car. One driver then followed the other, and we took several winding roads toward the campground.

Unfortunately, though, our rescuers were forced to drop us off at a railroad station a bit shy of our destination. Beyond the railroad tracks, the "road" to the campground was only a walkway.

That left Petey and me having to bike *one extra mile*—in complete darkness.

I offered the women some money for helping us out, but they refused to take it. They suggested that we instead pay it forward someday by helping someone else in need.

Before they left, I borrowed one of their cell phones to call Trevia and let her know we were alive and well. We then said goodbye to our team of angels and rode over the railroad tracks for that final mile until—at long last!—we arrived at the campground. Up ahead, I saw a silhouette of Trevia standing in front our cabin. It was one of our most joyful reunions ever!

We will never forget the kindness of the fellow human beings who came to our aid that day—providing water to quench our thirst, giving Trevia a lift and our backs a break, and driving us very close to our destination at no cost and with much enthusiasm.

But the people we met could only take us so far. We had to *go the extra mile* ourselves. No one could do it for us.

There will be times when our mental, emotional, and physical tanks will be empty. It's during these times that we need to dig deep and go the extra mile—for our customers or clients; for our friends; and, most importantly, for our families. It will be tough sometimes, but it will always be worth it.

Petey's (and our) task that day was more than a mere bike ride for me. It elevated my expectations. It helped me experience the goodness of others—and it helped our family see the power of working together, communicating through a crisis, and finding a way to succeed.

BEAUTY AMID THE MUD

by Peter Colwell

When life gets upended and goals get suspended
It's easy to wave the white flag
To just call it quits at the end of your wits
when everything feels like a drag.

With so much anxiety within our society,
It's tempting to go off the rails.
But let's gain perspective and be more reflective
Remembering that love never fails.

Amid all the mud that gets splashed in our face
Lies a *beautiful* treasure—our saving grace;
Persistent belief in our will to win
Resistance to pressure for us to give in

Compassion for others who fight the good fight
Wisdom that helps us to see the light
Relentless pursuit of a happy existence
Courage to finally go the distance!

3

KEY TAKEAWAYS
from Chapter Five

1. Spell out your long-term goals and put your vision into print.

2. Be true to your purpose and align your expectations with it.

3. You have to go the extra mile yourself. It will always be worth it.

An Attitude
of Abundance

by Peter Colwell

Cultivate peace in your heart and your mind
And sooner or later you're likely to find
That all of your trouble and worry and care
Can be kept in perspective if only you'll dare

To dream of a life overflowing with laughter
With hope for the future and the joy that you're after.

Choose your response to any circumstance
Don't leave a positive outcome to chance.

Take action to shape your life's direction.
Accentuate kindness, love, and affection.

Navigate through negative emotions with care.
Of people who drain you and strain you ... BEWARE!

Grow from your experiences each day of your life.
Learn from each setback, each heartache and strife.

Expect more out of life. You get what you give.
Now is the time to WAKE UP AND LIVE!

chapter six

Invest in Your Attitude

There is a destiny that makes us [sisters and] brothers:
None goes his way alone:
All that we send into the lives of others
Comes back into our own.

EDWIN MARKHAM

When all is said and done, our life is shaped by our thoughts, our beliefs and experiences, and **what we do with what we've discovered** (about ourselves and others) along the way.

Will we take the necessary actions to move forward? Will we get ourselves into a resourceful frame of mind so that we can implement positive, productive changes in our lives? Will we stretch ourselves from time to time and take chances to catapult our careers, enrich our spirits, and expand our vision of what's possible?

As we continue to navigate a global pandemic that has upended the world as we knew it, and as we face a new frontier with fortitude and fear, let's embrace what is good in the world and be the light we wish to see—a beacon of hope for others.

May our legacy be one of faith and resilience, laughter and goodwill, compassion and kindness. May our mindset lift us to new heights and help us envision brighter days on the horizon. And may we take time each day to invest in our most valuable and powerful asset—our attitude!

Invest in Your Attitude

by Peter Colwell

Do thy spirits need a lift?
Are your goals and dreams adrift?
Swirling loose without a rudder?
Causing you to spin and sputter?

Stumbling, grumbling ... getting by?
Hoping, coping ... wondering why
Life moves at such a turtle's pace?
"Slow and steady ... wins the race!"

Investing in our attitude
Is one way faith can be renewed
By dwelling on what brings us light
We daily build our strength and might

Each day we grow in grace and grit
Until we find our perfect fit
A flame emerging from a spark
Allowing us to make our mark!

A Fellow Traveler

Afterword by Peter Vogt, Editor

One year—almost to the day—before Peter Colwell and I finished editing this book together, he quit his job, without having another one lined up. His reason? The job was not a good fit for his values.

He elaborated in an email to me:

I'm learning how to "navigate through negativity."

You might remember that phrase; it's the theme (and the title) of Chapter Three.

Nine months before Peter Colwell and I finished editing this book together, he held his beautiful mother Marjorie's hand as she passed away from pancreatic cancer. His work on the book was understandably delayed. But the work he did on *himself*, using the very tools and concepts you've been reading about here, continued unabated. In fact, it escalated.

Three months before Peter Colwell and I finished editing this book together, his wife, Trevia, was in a serious car accident. Thankfully she wasn't badly hurt, nor was anyone else. The car, however, didn't fare so well. So, fearing that their ten-year-old Hyundai Elantra would be declared a total loss, Peter and Trevia decided to clean out its glovebox before the tow truck arrived to take the car away.

As they dug through the compartment's items, they came upon something truly amazing: an old copy of Peter's poem "An Attitude of Abundance"—which, as you might also remember, is the poem that ends Chapter Five in this book.

Peter's response, in an email sharing the tale (and notifying me of another understandable delay!), was equally amazing:

Reading my poem a few times intentionally helped put me in a better frame of mind, and we all (despite being shaken up) were able to eventually get back to our happy place. It takes work to get there: a choice to find the silver lining; determination that we will figure things out (eventually); a mindset adjustment (what's next vs. what was); sifting through the tough—but natural—emotions; debriefing and learning from the experience (how can we put it in perspective?); and getting genuinely excited about the prospect of a new(er) car—maybe leasing instead of buying ... elevating our expectations! We put the incident behind us and enjoyed an afternoon of tennis at [son] Petey's high school!

He then ended the email with this:

In retrospect, we ran through all the *Invest in Your Attitude* steps—with or without realizing it!

I have known Peter Colwell for twenty years now, without ever having met him face to face (yet!). I don't need to, though, in order to tell you what I'm about to tell you—perhaps the most important thing a self-help reader should know about his/her book's author:

Peter uses his own stuff.

That is to say: Peter's ideas are road-tested not only on other people, but also on himself. By himself. Peter uses his own stuff. Because he wants to? Maybe. But it's really because he has to—just like the rest of us.

So as you digest what Peter has written about in *Invest in Your Attitude*, know that he is not sailing painlessly above the fray. He's investing in his attitude too. Every. Single. Day. He's in the trenches with you. He is living life, the same as the rest of us are, with all its highs *and* lows.

Look, then, at what you've learned here as exactly what it is: the mindset and tools and strategies and wisdom not of a distant expert or pie-in-the-sky guru, but of a fellow traveler. A real fellow traveler. One who's walking with you.

May your investment bring you many happy returns!

About the Author

Peter Colwell is an artist of the written and spoken word whose mission in life is to uplift and inspire others. A native of Boston and a lifelong Boston Celtics fan, Peter holds a bachelor of science degree in languages and linguistics from Georgetown University. He is a certified trainer of the "Dale Carnegie Skills for Success Course" and creator of an award-winning leadership development program for a Fortune 500 company. 

Peter has held management and leadership positions in real estate and property management for nearly two decades and is the author of *Spell SUCCESS in Your Life: A Roadmap for Achieving Your Goals and Surviving Success*, which became a nonfiction bestseller in India and has been published in eight countries. Peter is also a professional member of the National Speakers Association and its Washington, DC chapter.

Peter is the lucky husband of Trevia-Lynne Colwell and the proud daddy of Petey and Vanessa Colwell. When he's not writing poems or giving motivational talks, he can be found shooting hoops, going for hikes, or catching up on the latest Netflix show with his family.

For more information, visit:

PeterColwell.com

About the Editor

I'm *The Introvert Advocate.*

If you're an introvert, I can help you to simply be who you are in this very extraverted world of ours. No more justifying. No more defending. No more apologizing. Only occasional explaining!

This is what I believe:

- You *deserve* to just go ahead and be the introvert you are.

- You *need* to be the introvert you are to be truly healthy and happy in life.

- You *can* be the introvert you are, even if you might sometimes think otherwise.

- With the right knowledge, the right practical tools, and the right mindset ... you WILL!

Note: I also, very occasionally, edit books that speak to me personally and that, much more importantly, have something critical to offer the world. *Invest in Your Attitude* (and Peter Colwell) qualifies times two!

To learn more about my work with introverts—and/or to sign up for my free monthly, printed-and-mailed newsletter, *Introvert Insights*—visit: **IntrovertInsights.com**

Thanks!

Peter Vogt

Made in the USA
Middletown, DE
07 September 2021

47773551R00106